Praise for
How to Talk to Your Kids about Your Divorce

"Solid gold advice. With years of experience guiding parents during and after divorce, Dr. Rodman has distilled her knowledge into a down-to-earth, practical, and well-grounded guide. If you want to be prepared for the toughest issues and ensure your children's psychological health, get one copy for yourself and one for your ex and keep it handy. You will return to it many times."
—Dr. Richard A. Warshak, author of *Divorce Poison*

"Divorce sucks, plain and simple. But this straightforward and honest guide to helping your kids through it will no doubt make it suck less. And making the tough times suck less is pretty much the best we can do."
—Jill Smokler, *New York Times* bestselling author of *Confessions of a Scary Mommy*

"Dr. Samantha Rodman has written a wonderful book that every divorcing parent should read. Breaking the news to your children in an emotionally attuned way is only the beginning. How to follow that up with empathy, the right words, and awareness of each child's individual needs is explained and made easy to read. Dr. Rodman offers a combination of down-to-earth language, practical examples, and professional acumen that is rare in self-help books."
—Jonice Webb, PhD, author of *Running on Empty: Overcome Your Childhood Emotional Neglect*

"*How to Talk to Your Kids about Your Divorce* is a richly informative book and a go-to guide for parents coping with divorce. Dr. Samantha Rodman helps bring light to how children feel while moving through this difficult process and offers tips, techniques, and healing approaches with warmth and wisdom. This book will help children feel heard and loved and will help anchor parents as they wade through the tides and turns their new lives will bring."
—Dr. Deborah Serani, author of *Depression and Your Child*

"*How to Talk to Your Kids about Your Divorce* is a straightforward and comprehensive guide to the challenging transitions that di   bring. With sensitivity, expertise, and real-life examples, Dr. Rodman   process and its effects on the family. It's an indispensable s   our children
—Andrea Bonior, PhD, *www.thefriendsl*

Praise for
How to Talk to Your Kids about Your Divorce

"If you are thinking about getting divorced, are getting divorced, or have been divorced, . . . you must read this book. Especially if you are dealing with an unreasonable ex, this book will help immensely. Dr. Samantha Rodman speaks the truth in a very direct and very compassionate manner. If your children and their mental health mean anything to you, read this book and take her advice."
—Marina Sbrochi, author of *Stop Looking for a Husband: Find the Love of Your Life* and, out soon, *Nasty Divorce: A Kid's Eye View*, *www.nastydivorcekidseyeview.com*

"A thorough and accessible book for parents. Dr. Rodman's practical and age-appropriate advice will open lines of communication about everything from sadness to anger to disappointment to fear. She takes you through the whole gamut of possible challenges a parent might face. Use her guidelines and you *will* parent well through the complexity of divorce."
—Jenny Kanevsky, regular contributor on parenting and divorce at the *Huffington Post* and The Good Men Project, *http://jennykanevsky.com*

"Dr. Rodman has provided insightful and very informative examples and advice for all parents covering every stage of separation and divorce. As a family law attorney, I believe if all of my clients and their counterparts going through custody matters read this book, it could very likely save them and their families the emotional turmoil that occurs during a contested legal battle, as well as time and money. Most importantly, *How to Talk to Your Kids about Your Divorce* will help families reach the best possible outcome for both parents and their children."
—Evan M. Koslow, Esq., family law attorney

Healthy, Effective Communication Techniques for Your Changing Family

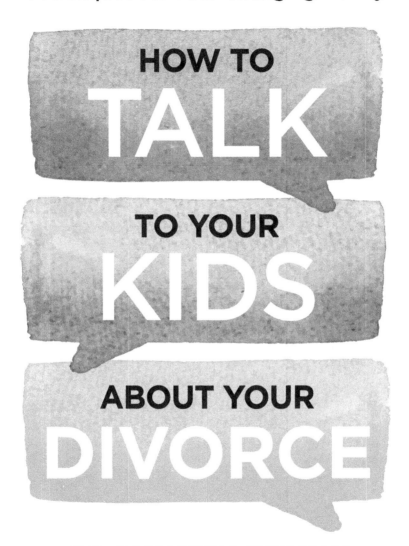

HOW TO
TALK
TO YOUR
KIDS
ABOUT YOUR
DIVORCE

DR. SAMANTHA RODMAN
Founder of DrPsychMom.com

Adams Media
New York London Toronto Sydney New Delhi

Adams Media
An Imprint of Simon & Schuster, Inc.
57 Littlefield Street
Avon, Massachusetts 02322

For information about special discounts for bulk purchases, please contact Simon & Schuster Special Sales at 1-866-506-1949 or business@simonandschuster.com.

The Simon & Schuster Speakers Bureau can bring authors to your live event. For more information or to book an event contact the Simon & Schuster Speakers Bureau at 1-866-248-3049 or visit our website at www.simonspeakers.com.

Interior images © iStockphoto.com/sunnysideeggs.

Manufactured in the United States of America

10 9 8 7 6 5 4 3 2

Library of Congress Cataloging-in-Publication Data has been applied for.

ISBN 978-1-4405-8878-5
ISBN 978-1-4405-8879-2 (ebook)

DEDICATION

This book is dedicated to my husband and children
for their love and support, and to my readers and
clients for sharing their experiences with me.

ACKNOWLEDGMENTS

This book would not be possible without the help and support from Jacqueline Musser and Shannon Smith at Adams Media and the inspiring work of all authors and researchers cited in this book.

CONTENTS

INTRODUCTION

If you're reading this book, it's because you're struggling with the idea or the reality of divorce, and concerned about the impact it will have on your children. First, let me say how sorry I am that you're in this place. An extensive history of marital conflict, disappointment, and hurt usually precedes one or both partners deciding to divorce. Divorce is one of life's most painful and harrowing experiences, and, according to research, only the death of a spouse is more stressful. (And I would be willing to bet that divorce can take the number-one place in many circumstances.)

No matter how many other issues are racing through your mind right now—and there are likely more than you can count—you've chosen to set aside time to read a book on communicating with your kids about divorce. This indicates that you're fully committed to maintaining the psychological and emotional wellbeing of your children during this difficult time, and that you want to minimize the disruption and pain that your divorce will cause. As a psychologist, I commend you on taking this step to proactively work on easing your children's distress about your divorce. Many parents avoid thinking about the painful reality of their children's anxiety and confusion during this process, and just hope for the best. Unfortunately, a less proactive approach often means that children have no idea what is happening, and end up feeling lost, betrayed, and angry.

Thankfully, there are many concrete tools that you can use in order to communicate effectively with your children about the topics of separation and divorce, whether they are toddlers only starting to talk, elementary-school age, or teenagers. This book aims to reduce your stress in at least this one area; if you know that you're facilitating open and developmentally appropriate communication with your kids, you can feel confident that you have tried your hardest to help them through this difficult process. These tools are simple and straightforward, and, best of all, they can be used to communicate with kids about any topic, not only divorce.

Whether or not your co-parent reads this book, or is on board with the advice that it gives, you can still use it very effectively to help yourself and your child have a healthier and more open relationship. Of course, the stress of conflict with your co-parent cannot be overstated, and this book will also cover ways to decrease some of this conflict. Although it's easier said than done, if you are able to feel more positive, or even more neutral, toward your co-parent, this can be perhaps the most important thing that you do for the psychological wellbeing of your children.

This book will also include many anonymized questions, quotes, and examples from real-life veterans of divorce and adult children of divorce, the readers of DrPsychMom.com, and examples I have fictionalized that touch upon issues I have discussed over the years with clients going through divorces. These examples provide glimpses of the experiences of people who have been in the trenches of separation and divorce. Hopefully, they will resonate with your personal experiences, and help give voice to your own struggles.

By the end of this book, you'll be able to:

- Understand what children commonly feel when their parents divorce

- Discuss divorce-related topics (e.g., separate homes, visits, why this happened) in age-appropriate ways with your child

- Initiate conversations where your children can feel safe in expressing their honest feelings about the divorce

- Realize the dangers of confiding too deeply in your child, and change this dynamic
- Know when and how to get help for your own divorce-related emotional struggles
- Know how emotions work, and how to teach emotional awareness and acceptance to your child
- Understand how children may express their feelings in different ways, based on their ages and personalities
- Empathize with your child's experience without trying to "fix" or minimize it
- Validate your child's feelings, making your child feel safe and secure
- Understand why I keep referring to your ex-spouse as a "co-parent" throughout this book, and why it's so important to use this term yourself
- Understand the difference between forcing your children to communicate and allowing them the space to come to you
- Feel confident that you've opened up the lines of communication with your child, not only about divorce, but about all difficult or sensitive issues
- Discuss hot-button topics with your child without losing your cool
- Incorporate more positive bonding activities into your post-divorce life with your child
- Realize that your divorce will not break your child, and realize that the way you talk about the divorce may actually strengthen and deepen your relationship with your child

I see many adult clients who were children of divorce, and for every one that felt traumatized by the divorce, there is one who feels that, in fact, the divorce was a positive thing, as the child ended up with two happier parents, and often, loving stepparents. The common denominators among happy and well-adjusted adult children of divorce are that they did not feel ignored, caught in the middle of sparring parents, or expected or forced to act or feel a certain way. Their perspectives and emotions were heard and understood rather than minimized, denied, or devalued, and their preferences were taken into account in developmentally appropriate ways. These are worthy goals for any divorcing parent—to try your hardest to make your child feel heard, acknowledged, prioritized, and safe.

Note: Throughout this book, male and female pronouns will be used interchangeably. Unless otherwise specified, the issues discussed apply to both male and female children. Additionally, there are specific times that I recommend seeking help from a therapist. By this, I mean a trained professional—a psychologist, social worker, or licensed counselor—who preferably has experience working with divorcing families. Even if I do not explicitly recommend counseling for an issue you may be going through, please always seek counseling if you feel that it is necessary to help you and your child through a particularly challenging time. Now, let's begin setting the stage for understanding how to communicate with your child about your divorce.

PART 1

Talking about Divorce

In the first part of this book, we will be preparing you to learn to communicate with and understand your child in new ways. We will cover types of divorce, how spoken language can change how you and your child feel about the divorce, and ways to ensure that your relationship with your child maintains appropriate boundaries amidst the chaos of divorce. This section also addresses the unique influence of divorce on different kids' personality types and offers a basic primer about the critical role of emotional expression and acceptance in helping your child cope and heal. These seven chapters will give you a broad overview of everything to look out for as you and your child embark on (or continue) the journey of creating your post-divorce family.

CHAPTER 1

DIVORCE: NOT ONE-SIZE-FITS-ALL

*"All happy families are alike; each unhappy
family is unhappy in its own way."*
—*Anna Karenina* by Leo Tolstoy

Divorce is not a one-size-fits-all construct. The relationship between spouses and, later, co-parents, the amount and type of conflict in the marriage and in the divorce, the relationship between each parent and each child, and the relationship between siblings can all influence how children are affected by their parents' divorce.

TYPES OF UNHAPPY MARRIAGES

There are many issues that can contribute to the dissolution of a marriage, including, but not limited to: infidelity (physical and/or emotional); lack of emotional connection; opposing ideas about major household issues (finances, parenting, work-life balance, involvement of grandparents); and issues related to mental and emotional health (addiction, mood and anxiety disorders, personality-level variables, co-dependency). Despite the range of reasons that your marriage may have ended, your children often only notice one variable—whether or not they have witnessed extensive open conflict. Therefore, we will classify unhappy marriages into two main types: ones where the conflict is right out in the open, and ones where it is hidden, either behind closed doors or not even discussed by the spouses themselves.

The Openly Conflictual Home

In this marriage, there is open and acrimonious fighting. There is yelling, threatening, and arguing, and possibly violence between spouses. Parents may insult one another, or act contemptuous or dismissive of one another. Often, at least one parent badmouths the other to the children, or engages in passive-aggressive behavior like rolling their eyes when the other parent talks, or undermining one another's parenting decisions. Old problems are endlessly rehashed, including such issues as infidelity, disagreements about finances, or difficulties with in-laws. These arguments occur either directly in front of the kids or when the kids are "asleep" (but they hear it anyway). The word *divorce* may have been used, and more than once, within the kids' earshot. Sometimes there is no physical affection, and sometimes there is unpredictable physical affection, and even passion, since volatile relationships often are characterized by high highs and low lows. This latter situation can be even more confusing for children, as they never know whether Mom and Dad love each other or not, and may learn to associate physical intimacy with fear or conflict.

The children in these families can respond in a variety of ways to this constant conflict. Sometimes all the children take their cue from the oldest child, and sometimes siblings respond differently. There are typical ways that children respond to conflict in the home, and they represent different coping styles that they have developed with the unconscious or conscious goal of making their situation better—either by limiting its impact on them or by changing or fixing the problems between their parents.

Some children ignore the conflict entirely, no matter how loud or violent the fighting gets. Parents may tell themselves that this means that their children don't notice or aren't affected by the conflict. However, despite their outward appearance of not caring, these children are learning that this conflict is what it means to be in a relationship. They often exhibit the same stress reactions as other children, but parents don't link these to the conflict in the home, since these children appear not to react to the fighting.

Other children take sides, defending and comforting one parent and blaming and demonizing the other. They may be used to viewing one parent as the victim and one as the perpetrator in the frequent arguments. They may say "Leave Mommy alone" to their father or roll their eyes at their mother when she "comes after" Dad. A pattern where one parent and one or all children stand together against another parent is called *triangulation*, and can be very toxic to the kids' emotional health. This is an early precursor to children reviling one parent after a divorce (parental alienation, as discussed in Chapter 7).

Another often-seen dynamic is where children try to repair the relationship between their parents. They explain one parent's viewpoint to the other and try to smooth over conflicts. Sometimes a child will take a comedian role, hoping to lessen tension between parents by cracking jokes. Other kids become troublemakers with the same unconscious goal: distracting their parents from fighting. This can temporarily work, as parents come together to discipline or complain about their child's misbehavior. It is noteworthy and shows how difficult marital conflict is on a child that a child generally wants his parents to get along even more than he wants them to approve of his behavior.

In some openly conflictual households, some children (particularly older siblings, or oldest female children; see Chapter 4) act older than their years. They may try to shield younger ones from the fighting, or care for younger siblings when parents' distress renders them unable to function appropriately as caretakers. They may feed or bathe younger siblings, do homework with them, or put them to bed. Children in openly conflictual homes also can become *parentified*, a psychological term which means that they act as a parent to their own parent, taking care of them emotionally or even fixing them meals or cleaning the house when a parent feels too distressed to function. They may also take on a confidante-like role with one or both parents (see Chapter 3), where they provide comfort and a shoulder to lean on for a parent who is struggling. Such parents feel so lonely and distraught that they welcome any caretaking behavior, even when they know that their children should not be providing this sort of comfort.

Whether or not the children acknowledge and respond to the marital discord in an openly conflictual home, it is likely that they are exhibiting some stress-related reactions, like anxiety, anger, acting out in school, sleep problems, inability to focus on schoolwork, and interpersonal issues with peers. They are soaking everything up, and learning that conflict and dissatisfaction are the basis of a marriage. This is a lesson that is very hard to unlearn, since it is absorbed on such an unconscious level at a formative developmental stage.

Children in an openly conflictual home have more forewarning that their parents may divorce, since they may have overheard threats about divorce during arguments, or they may be old enough to know that fighting can lead to divorce. Still, the news that their parents are actually divorcing will be painful and surprising. Kids cherish fantasies that, one day, their parents will just start to get along, and everyone will be happy. Knowing that this will never happen is like a punch in the gut, no matter how unhappy the household has been. However, long term, if their post-divorce life becomes calmer and more stable than their pre-divorce life, kids in this situation may feel that their parents made the right choice for everyone.

It is normal to feel guilty after reading the description of an openly conflictual marriage. While it is true that being exposed to constant fighting, anger, and bitterness is bad for children's mental and even physical health, you cannot change the past, and it is a good thing that you were brave enough to move forward with divorce. Now your kids will have a chance to realize that the patterns they saw in your household were not representative of a healthy marriage. You can discuss what they saw, and explain that your marriage wasn't healthy. Moreover, you can commit to changing these patterns from this point forward, in your post-divorce family and relationships.

The Secretly Unhappy Home

This family is very different from the openly conflictual home. On the surface it looks like a happy family, headed up by a couple that is loving and even affectionate. But this is not what is going on underneath. In this relationship, although parents put on a happy face in front of everyone, including their kids, the spouses feel lonely and despondent.

Sometimes I think of these types of couples as "divorced in spirit." Often, the partners sleep in separate rooms and have no intimacy or physical contact. Despite this, their kids may have no idea that their parents are not in love, and only later on (such as in therapy) will they note that they never saw their parents kiss or touch. They often don't think this is abnormal, having grown up with it, and they assume that if there was any conflict between their parents, there would have been open fighting.

A secretly unhappy marriage can keep on trucking for a long time, because both partners are emotionally avoidant and hate confrontation. If one partner asks for a divorce, it's usually due to some major life change, like starting a new job, starting therapy, or, of course, starting another romantic relationship. The other partner, who was equally unhappy but may have made peace with remaining in an unhappy marriage for the sake of the kids, finances, or any other reason, may now feel extremely angry and betrayed. This is how a secretly unhappy marriage can lead to a high-conflict divorce.

Kids with parents in secretly unhappy marriages will be completely blindsided by a divorce. These children often feel very secure about their parents' relationship, and may have even felt lucky to have a non-divorced and loving family, distinguishing them from their classmates with divorced parents. No matter their ages, the children will be extremely confused and feel shaken to the core, because, as far as everyone knew, there were no problems at all. In *A Generation at Risk: Growing Up in an Era of Family Upheaval* (1997), authors Paul R. Amato and Alan Booth discuss that, post-divorce, children of low-conflict marriages have worse outcomes as adults than children of high-conflict marriages, due to issues with trust and intimacy.

Additionally, if you've tried to keep your marital conflict hidden from your children, they may wonder what else you've been keeping hidden. Issues of trust may emerge, particularly for older kids or teens, who may wonder if anything else, or everything else, in their lives was a lie. In this situation, kids have no idea what to think, and often, their anger and confusion can manifest against one parent in particular, whichever one they can more easily blame. For example, a teenager may think, "It must be Dad's fault. I know he worked so much and I bet Mom was lonely."

In secretly unhappy marriages that lead to divorce, there may be more questions from the children than in openly conflictual marriages. As we will discuss in subsequent chapters, these questions must be addressed honestly and respectfully, as the children have a right to know developmentally appropriate information about why their family is breaking up.

Addiction and Mental Illness

A particularly heartbreaking type of openly conflictual marriage is a marriage where one or both parents struggle with addiction or mental illness. These issues can render parents unable to effectively care for themselves and their children. Their judgment is compromised, and younger children may not have any idea why their parents are so unpredictable and scary. Families in which one or both parents suffer from addiction or mental illness can fall into either category of marriage headed toward divorce—openly conflictual or secretly unhappy. For example, alcoholic parents may fight loudly and violently in front of their children, or one parent may be distant and detached, drinking alone out of the kids' sight. Similarly, a parent with bipolar disorder may have unpredictable and volatile anger issues while a parent with depression may spend time lying silently on the couch. Again, the more that open conflict occurs, the likelier the children will be to have some inkling that a divorce may be on the horizon (unless the children are very young), but it will likely still be shocking and painful. We will discuss the unique issues associated with mental illness and addiction in Chapter 7.

THREE TYPES OF DIVORCE

I have observed three different types of divorce among the couples that I see in treatment: amicable, strained, and high-conflict. They each have a specific impact on the children's ability to cope and thrive post-divorce. Sadly, according to Amato and Booth in *A Generation at Risk,* 30 percent of divorces are considered "high conflict" and up to 60 percent are considered "moderate to high conflict," so amicable divorces are in the minority. Learning about what type of divorce you are going through can help you understand how your children will react and why.

The Amicable Divorce

In this situation, the divorce was mutually agreed upon and was likely years in the making. Both spouses are still friends but are not in love anymore. Usually, this is not a situation where there was domestic violence, infidelity, or extensive dishonesty. It usually results from a secretly unhappy home or marriage where the conflict was hidden or contained. Often, both spouses have a social support network of friends and family, and/or their own therapists. These buffers allow them to be magnanimous with each other, and to pin the "blame" for the divorce on their situation or lack of compatibility, not just the other partner's perceived deficiencies.

This is a best-case scenario and is fairly uncommon. While the children certainly suffer and mourn the loss of their non-divorced family, they do not have to simultaneously contend with parental anger and bitterness. They are not exposed to parents trash-talking one another, which allows them to remain emotionally close with both parents. This is the best outcome a child of divorce can hope for.

The Strained Divorce

In this scenario, which is much more common, both spouses feel some animosity and bitterness, but this can be contained, particularly in front of the children. There is no overwhelming hatred, and each spouse can see the other's positive qualities, at least some of the time. In this situation, the children can remain emotionally healthy and happy, after a period during which they grieve their family's breakup and acclimate to new routines. The more they are shielded from what anger and resentment does remain between the parents, the better they can cope.

The High-Conflict Divorce

In this sad situation, a couple cannot agree upon anything in terms of co-parenting, finances, living arrangements, and so forth. There is often a history of dishonesty and infidelity, and at least one spouse feels like the victim in the marriage. The exes continue to argue in front of the kids as much as, if not more than, they did when they were married.

Children find it very difficult to thrive in this type of divorce. They feel forced to take sides, and to blame one parent for the fighting and hostility. Kids will often develop psychological, emotional, and even physical problems from the stress of living in this type of environment. A phone call from one parent can send the other into a rage. Pickups and drop-offs are fraught with tension, snide remarks, and accusations. This is the worst of both worlds—the parents are no longer together, but the children still cannot escape the conflict.

A man undergoing a high-conflict divorce may think something like this: "My wife goes out and parties like she has no kids. No wonder the kids look anxious when it's time to go back to Mom's house. I wish I could go back in time and leave the marriage sooner. Those years I will never get back. Every time I talk to her, my blood pressure goes up."

If you and your co-parent fall into one of the first two categories, it is likely that the tips in this book may provide you with the communication skills necessary to connect more effectively with your children during this difficult time. Co-parents who still respect one another, and who do not have a history of violence or volatility can more easily move into a co-parenting relationship that puts the children first.

However, many couples have arrived at the decision to divorce at the end of a long road of contentious, violent, and devastating conflict, throughout which they have experienced intense feelings of betrayal, hatred, and rage. If you're in a high-conflict divorce like this, I highly recommend that you look for a counselor who can help you learn coping strategies to manage your emotions, particularly in front of your children. Anger, resentment, and anxiety can come to the surface in frequent, open conflict. This conflict is toxic for children to witness and will have permanent negative effects on their psychological health, including their later capacity to form trusting intimate relationships as adults. Furthermore, stress may be a trigger for the development of underlying mental and emotional issues in children with predispositions toward these issues.

Many parents think that conflict with their co-parent will abate in a few months. However, in *The Unexpected Legacy of Divorce: A 25 Year Landmark Study*, by Judith S. Wallerstein, Julia M. Lewis, and Sandra Blakeslee, the authors maintain that a third of divorced couples are still fighting with the same intensity a decade after their divorce. Adult clients often recall horribly stressful interactions between their divorced parents, from verbal sniping at school functions to open scenes at birthday parties, weddings, and even much later events, such as celebrations for grandchildren born decades after a divorce. Nor does the addition of a new partner for one or both of the divorced parents lead to a cease-fire. Many times, the introduction of new partners brings up or exacerbates feelings of jealousy and anger, particularly insofar as the new arrangement affects finances and the treatment of children.

WHEN TO GET HELP

If you have lost your temper frequently with your co-parent in front of your children, the first order of business must be working with a trained professional in order to get you to a healthier emotional place. Even if you're in bad financial circumstances, there are many therapists with sliding-scale fees, and even therapists who take pro bono cases. You can find psychologists and counselors who provide therapy for free by researching "pro bono therapy" in your area. A therapist is not only someone who can teach you concrete skills for dealing with your anger and guilt. He or she can also be an emotional support, a safe place to vent your thoughts and feelings, and someone who treats you with respect and care. Therapy can be an oasis during a very stressful time in your life.

In addition to working with a therapist, you may also be able to find very helpful support groups for separated and divorced individuals, which can provide a safe space to talk about your divorce and your struggles with your co-parent. We will discuss therapists and support groups more in the section "Appropriate Confidantes" in Chapter 3, as well as the techniques used in acceptance and commitment therapy, a particularly helpful form of therapy for learning to accept and move past your negative emotions, in Chapter 5.

Medication management can also be a useful adjunct to therapy. If you feel irritable, angry, anxious, or tearful; if you are unable to accept joy into your life; if you can't focus at work or home; if you are unable to engage in self-care (eating well, sleeping, exercising); you may be experiencing symptoms of depression. At the very least, you are likely experiencing an adjustment disorder due to the upheaval and chaos of your divorce. Many divorcing individuals find it useful to speak to a psychiatrist who can evaluate your need for antidepressant or antianxiety medications. Another route to regaining equilibrium can be exercise, mindfulness meditation, or working with an alternative healing provider if this is your preference. Of course, reading this book and others on divorce will be helpful as well, particularly the sections on recognizing, accepting, and processing feelings.

It is important to realize that if your emotions are frequently out of hand in front of your children, seeking help no longer becomes a matter of preference. You must move past your shame, guilt, and denial to acknowledge and address your behavior. Whether or not you personally have felt comfortable with the idea of therapy or medication in the past is much less important than whether these strategies enable you to be a more functional parent to your child. The priority is making sure that your child feels safe and supported during your divorce, which is particularly challenging since you yourself likely feel devastated as well. It is essential to do everything that you can to strengthen yourself emotionally to be the parent that your child needs right now.

If you can engage in self-reflection and objectively examine your current emotional functioning and its impact on your parenting, you can significantly improve your relationship with your child during this difficult time. In fact, you may even end up having a closer relationship with your child than you had before marital conflict and/or the stress of separation. By using the communication skills we will learn in Chapter 6, as well as prioritizing quality time with your child and making yourself available to him, as we will discuss in Chapter 14, you can facilitate the most secure and loving relationship possible with your child. Your healthy parent-child relationship will be a buffer to help your child deal more effectively with the stressors of the divorce.

SIBLING RELATIONSHIPS

Siblings can be a wonderful resource for each other in times of stress. There are many adult children of divorce who have tender memories of siblings serving as friends, confidantes, and protectors during times of conflict and tension in the home. If your children are already close, they will likely be more resilient during your divorce. They have each other to turn to, so at least that relationship stays constant, and likely will grow even stronger.

Unfortunately, some siblings also are sworn enemies. Sibling bullying is real, and in relationships where siblings already do not get along, a divorce can make things even worse. Parents are consumed with their own stress, and often fail to intervene in sibling arguments or even physical altercations the way that they did before the divorce. In the absence of parental supervision, sibling conflict can often escalate out of control, and relationships can be permanently ruined.

I Hated My Brother

Larry, 35, recalls that, after his parents' divorce when he was ten, his mother became depressed and started napping on the couch after work. It fell to him to take care of his 6-year-old brother, Michael, a difficult child with ADHD and oppositional behaviors. Larry felt that his brother was a burden, and that it was unfair that he had to bring his brother along when playing with friends or riding his bike. He found his brother disruptive and annoying, and was ashamed of his brother's behavior in front of his friends. Frequently, Larry would tease his brother, who became enraged and frustrated and would often lash out physically. This would make Larry tease him more for "throwing tantrums."

Larry and Michael both begged their mother to change their arrangement. Larry wanted to play sports after school and Michael just wanted more time with his mother. However, their mother was unable to acknowledge the seriousness of their entreaties and told them to "just get along" and "let Mommy rest."

Larry's relationship with his brother deteriorated over the course of their childhoods. In adulthood, they are cordial at family gatherings but never visit or call one another. Their resentment and anger never fully dissipated. Larry is still angry with his mother for ignoring how difficult it was for him to effectively parent his brother every afternoon for years. Michael, conversely, is angry at his father for not realizing that he was being bullied every afternoon, and for leaving his mother to deal with her depression on her own. The family is fractured.

Larry's mother did not intend to foster a sibling relationship that would end in adulthood estrangement. She felt depressed and overwhelmed, and told herself that "boys will be boys," minimizing the severity of the sibling conflict in her own mind. She was too emotionally exhausted to deal with the idea of enrolling the boys in afterschool programs and felt ashamed to ask the boys' father to take them for more hours. She told herself that the boys did not mean it when they said they hated one another, and felt that siblings "have to" love each other no matter what.

This situation could have been greatly helped by Larry's mother understanding that siblings do not "have to" love one another. Bullying between siblings can be equally as severe as any other bullying, and many children react poorly to feeling burdened with adult-level responsibilities, such as childcare. This sad story is an illustration of how important it is to take sibling conflict seriously, intervening when conflict never seems to resolve or when a child tells you repeatedly how upset he is by a sibling's behavior.

Overall, what matters most to kids of divorce is their ability to maintain loving, secure relationships with all members of their original family unit, including both parents, siblings, and extended families on both sides (if these relatives were close to the children prior to the divorce). The particulars of living situations, financial changes, and other arrangements are nowhere near as important for children as the emotional security of feeling valued and cherished by both of their parents and their other family members. The communication skills you'll learn in later chapters will help you show your child that you truly value his needs and perspectives, and that you can be trusted to be non-judgmental, accepting, respectful, and receptive.

Key points from this chapter:

- Different types of marital conflict will have different effects on how your children perceive and respond to your divorce

- The tone of your divorce will have a great impact on your children

- Focus on putting your child first, and realize that your own emotional functioning directly affects that of your child

- Siblings can be resources and supports for one another, but they can also undermine each other's ability to cope if you don't monitor their behavior

- It is essential to maintain your child's relationship with both parents as well as other key family members

CHAPTER 2

THE LANGUAGE OF DIVORCE

Telling your kids that you're getting a divorce is heart-wrenching and terrifying. Beyond the initial announcement, it can be confusing to figure out how to discuss divorce-related topics on a daily basis without overwhelming or upsetting your child. First, this chapter will outline some simple points that you can make sure to cover during your announcement of the divorce. Then we will examine how to discuss issues and field questions that are likely to crop up during your first few conversations. We will discuss ways that you can change the language you use about divorce to help change your children's (and likely, your own) views about it. And lastly, we'll explore what you should do if you find yourself alone in your efforts to speak differently to your kids, with your co-parent still using conflictual and accusatory language.

THE INITIAL TALK

Most, if not all, children remember the first time they heard that their parents were getting a divorce. Nothing can stop this moment from being shocking and painful. However, if you plan ahead, you can make this initial talk less traumatic for your children. Your goals are to transmit information in a calm and loving way, to answer questions that your children may have, and to reassure your children that you and your co-parent love them deeply.

There are some logistical issues that you and your co-parent have to decide before the announcement. The children will need to know how they will be dividing time between parents, and what major changes will occur. Hopefully you have been able to decide some of these basic issues before telling your children about your divorce. If not, tell them what you do know, and state that you will tell them more as you figure it out. Unless there is significant hostility that would make it impossible for you and your co-parent to sit down together, your initial discussion about the divorce should involve both parents and all children. If you and your co-parent cannot reasonably and calmly interact with each other, try to plan ahead so that you're not contradicting each other in your individual talks. If this, too, is impossible, then just follow these guidelines on your own, ensuring that you mention frequently that your co-parent also loves the children very much.

Both parents should try to speak in a calm tone, without intense or out-of-control displays of emotion. The goal is to show that the divorce is the best choice for everyone, although it is a sad situation. Crying may be unavoidable, and can even show the child that you take the divorce seriously and understand how hard it will be. However, if a parent gets loud or loses control, it can scare the children and teach them to associate the divorce with fear and trauma.

Parents should back up one another in this discussion, and show a united front for the children. This situation is confusing enough for kids without having to witness a difference of opinion between their parents about key issues. If Mom says, "You'll live with me, mostly," and Dad says, "You'll split time with us," a child feels anxious not only because she doesn't know what will actually happen, but also because she senses that a big conflict is brewing over this issue.

Here are some more tips:

- Don't tell the children in advance that a discussion is coming up. They will be very anxious and ruminate about it. Instead, say, "Daddy/Mommy and I need to talk to you now," right before the talk.

- Tell all siblings at the same time, so that no child feels that they are less important than the others. Furthermore, knowing that your parents are divorcing is a large burden to carry alone, even for a few days or hours.

- Don't tell friends or family members about the divorce before you tell the children. Hearing about a divorce second hand is very upsetting for kids and can stop them from trusting you in the future.

- Don't have the discussion in a public place, where a child's reactions may embarrass him, or where he can't feel free to ask questions.

- Try to stay physically close to your kids, to comfort them. Small children can sit on your lap if they want. Older children may appreciate a hand on their shoulder.

- Do not have the discussion on a special occasion, like a holiday, which may ruin this holiday for your children in the future.

- Try to have the discussion when the kids aren't tired, sick, or hungry, so that they can process what's happening and they are not as emotionally volatile.

- Don't tell the kids at a time when you won't be there to process the information with them afterwards. Do not choose a weekday morning before they head to school, right before an activity, or bedtime.

- Don't have other people in the house or expect your child to interact with others right after the discussion. Your child may want privacy after the announcement.

- Don't use sarcasm. Small kids don't understand it, and it has no place in this discussion. Be respectful of the seriousness of this announcement for your child.

- Don't tell the children if you're not 100 percent sure that you're going to divorce. If you still feel you may reconcile with your spouse, you must say that you're "separating, which means living separately" rather than "divorcing."

POINTS TO HIT IN THE FIRST DISCUSSION

Let's lay out the major points that are important to hit in the initial divorce discussion. I will also include examples of common things that parents say that are not as helpful and should be avoided.

"Mommy and Daddy are getting a divorce."

It is important to say the word *divorce*, even to young children, because it gives them a name for what is happening. Things that can be named are not as scary. Older children can immediately understand more of what's happening, just by hearing this word spoken out loud. You want to say "divorce" within the first few sentences of the conversation. This helps children understand that this is something new and different, and they will be more likely to understand the context for everything that follows. If you give the backstory of why you're divorcing first, children may become confused and tune you out.

"Mom and Dad don't get along, and our marriage is not working out. We think it will be better for us to get divorced and live apart."

Honesty is essential, but do not burden children with developmentally inappropriate or overly detailed explanations, or ones that blame one parent for the divorce—even if that parent may objectively be responsible for the decision to end the marriage. Still, you must respect your child's need to understand what is going on, as a major grievance of many adult children of divorce is that they felt like nobody explained anything. If your child keeps asking why you don't get along, and what you fight about, you can say, "We don't get along about many things, and they are all adult problems." If the child says, "I know you fight about me," which is often true, as arguments about parenting are common, understand that your child may be asking if he caused the fighting. You can say, "Yes, we fight about parenting and other things, too. You never cause us to fight, we would argue anyway."

Do *not* give any specifics of your arguments that cast one spouse in a bad light, such as "Dad has a girlfriend" or "Mommy is mad at Daddy." There is a natural tendency to want kids to be on your side if you feel wronged, but blaming one parent is always a mistake, especially in this first discussion that will frame how your child may think of the divorce from this point onward. We will discuss how to talk about your co-parent in Chapter 7.

"It is nobody's fault."

I prefer this to the often-heard "It's not your fault." There is a great deal of psychological research on the suggestibility of children, which indicates that they can be influenced to a dramatic extent by what they are told, or even asked, by adults. Many kids may not conceive of the idea that the divorce could be their fault, particularly if they were hearing parents fight about other problems. But if a child is asked, "Do you think this is your fault?" this may lead him to think about the possibility for the first time. Of course, many children may think the divorce is their fault and not come right out and ask you, which is why you will state unequivocally that nobody is to blame.

Using the word "nobody" sets the stage for the idea that there is not one parent who is more to blame for the divorce. Whether or not you believe this, or even if your spouse initiated the divorce and you still wanted to remain married, the best case for your child is to see the divorce decision as a united front, with neither parent as the perpetrator or victim.

"We are sorry."

The news of divorce is a terrible blow to children. It is important to express your sorrow or regret so that it is obvious that you care about how difficult the divorce may be for your child. In the majority of cases, your child will be distressed by this news, even if the marriage has been openly conflictual and/or the child has thought a divorce might be coming. If you show your child that you are sad that you couldn't give him a non-divorced family, this shows that you're not minimizing his grief about losing the only family structure that he has known.

Additionally, if you're sad, this shows your child that the marriage was very important to you, and that you recognize how serious and important marriage and divorce are. You are not just throwing your child's life into disarray for superficial reasons. Older children might also want to hear "We worked on the marriage, but we couldn't fix it." Again, this shows that you know how important it is for your kids to be in a non-divorced family, and you tried hard to give them one, and you deeply regret that you could not make it work.

Even if you feel happy and relieved that your marriage is over, it's not appropriate to share this with your child. It's also not the time to put a positive spin on the divorce. It's not "better" to have two families in the mind of your child; it's worse. At some point in her later life, your child may well consider your divorce to be a good thing, but it is best for her to come to this awareness on her own. Particularly in the initial discussion, it is very invalidating to your child to hear that you consider the divorce to be positive. This framework does not give your child the space to process and grieve this tremendous change in her family. She may think that the only acceptable response to the divorce is to be happy about it, and since she doesn't feel this way, her three emotionally unhealthy choices are either to lie to you, lie to herself, or shut down entirely.

"We both love you, and will always be your parents."

It's vitally important to reassure your child that both parents still love him and will still be involved in his life. There is no amount of reassurance that is excessive in this situation. Tell your child that you love him, and you will always love him. Emphasize what a delightful child he is and how he brings you both happiness, even during this time of major stress. It is also good to say that having children was a good part of the marriage, so that your children know that they were conceived in love, or at least, that having children was considered a positive thing by both parents.

"You will have a home with both of us. On Mondays, Tuesdays, and Wednesdays you'll be here, and Thursdays, Fridays, Saturdays, you'll be at Dad's new house. Sundays you'll have some time with each of us."

Even if one parent lives with the child much more of the time, make sure to tell the child that he will have a home with the other parent as well. Specify the arrangement if you know it.

Do *not* say: "You'll be living with Mommy, but you'll visit Daddy" (or vice versa), because this diminishes the involvement of the parent who is the visitee. We will discuss this idea in the "Change of Terminology" section in Chapter 7.

COMMON QUESTIONS

There are certain key questions that children ask, or want to ask, aside from the major ones that were covered previously. Children will ask different questions depending on their age, but answers to the following questions can be tailored to the developmental stage of any child. Note that many of these questions will crop up again and again in the weeks and months following the divorce; some will even continue to come up for years.

Ideally, before sitting down with the children, you and your co-parent will read through all of these potential questions and answers, and the two of you will decide how you want to respond to each. Of course, the animosity and strong emotion that is likely overwhelming both of you may make such a calm and pre-planned discussion impossible. In this case, you may be reading these questions and answers long after you've already told your children about your divorce, and you may feel guilty for not addressing or for possibly mishandling some of these answers. However, even if you told your children about the divorce months or years ago, you can still go back and explain more. The wonderful thing about being a parent is that there is a very long "window of opportunity" for most major discussions. You can and will continue to talk about divorce and its ramifications for a long time to come, since it is a key feature of your child's life. Here are some questions that your children may have and some answers you may want to give them:

"Will I go to the same schools, activities, and camps?"

You can respond, "We will do our best to keep your routine the same; the same school, the same camps, and the same sports." This is the best case scenario, and if this is not true, or if this is undecided, tell your child as much information as you have. For example, you could say, "You'll still go to the same school, but we are not sure yet about swim lessons."

"Will I have the same friends?"

You can say, "We will try our best to keep up with playdates with school friends, although they may not always be at this house. You can see your friends on our street when you're living with Mom during the week, but you may make other friends when you live with Dad on the weekends."

"What should I tell people?"

Respond by saying, "You can tell people that your parents are getting divorced, and that you will have two homes now. You don't have to tell anyone anything unless it comes up, or you can tell your friends right away. The choice is yours."

"Was this my fault?"

The answer to this question is always, "Of course not! There is nothing you could have done to prevent this. We both love you very much. You are the best part of our marriage."

"Which parent is to blame?"

Regardless of how the marriage broke down, the answer here should be, "Nobody is to blame. We didn't get along anymore, and we both decided to divorce."

"Will you ever get back together?"

Even if you're unsure, "No, I'm sorry" works best when answering this question. You must try your best not to encourage the idea that your divorce is a temporary state. The fantasy that parents will reconcile is very powerful, and even adult children sometimes hope that this will happen with parents who have been divorced for decades. Your job is to ensure that your child can look forward to his new life, not be consumed with the idea that his previous life is retrievable.

"Do you love each other anymore?"

You can answer this honestly, but do not leave room for the child to hope that you will reconcile. A good answer is, "We will always love each other because we made you together. But we don't love each other like married people should." Another honest answer is, "No, we don't. We used to love each other and now we don't feel that way anymore." Always stress that you used to love each other, so that your child does not feel that her birth was a mistake or a regret.

"Did you ever love each other?"

Try not to see your marriage as black-and-white, remember the times you loved each other and respond with, "Yes, we did when we got married, and when we had you." If this is entirely a lie, then you can say, "We thought we did, but we realized that we didn't. We did have many good times together though." But try to leave open the possibility that you did feel love at one time. It is important for children to think of themselves as loved and wanted, and this is harder for them if they are visualizing a marriage that was already broken when they were born. Additionally, if a child feels that his birth was designed to fix a marriage, he will feel guilty that he has seemingly failed at this task.

In a secretly unhappy marriage (see Chapter 1), the kids will feel much more shocked about the news of divorce than in a home where there was a great deal of open conflict. While there is no need to go into details about how long you and your spouse were unhappy in your marriage, it would be crazy-making for you to pretend that everything had been happy all along. This would make your children feel that relationships are completely unpredictable, and can change from happy to irreparably broken overnight. In this case, say, "Dad and I were unhappy with each other for a long time, although we did have some good times, especially with you kids. Eventually, we realized we should split up since we were getting more and more unhappy."

"Do you still love me?"

Heartbreaking though this question may be, it is one children sometimes ask in the uncertainty that follows an announcement of divorce. Fortunately, you and your co-parent can respond with "We will always love you so much." This is the time to be open and expressive about your love for your child. He is experiencing so much confusion, sadness, shock, and anger that it is imperative that he does not doubt your love.

"Will you stop loving me?"

Many kids, especially young ones, think that if parents stopped loving one another, they can just as easily and quickly stop loving their kids. Whether or not your child asks this question outright, it is a good idea to say, "Parents love kids forever. We could never stop loving you no matter what."

Again, even if you have already told your children about your divorce, you can go back and answer any of these questions, or start a discussion again, saying, "I'm just wondering if you guys had any more questions about the divorce. I know the first time we talked about it, it was surprising and you may not have been able to think of everything you wanted to ask." This is a good way to leave the lines of communication open and show your children that they do not have to be afraid to bring up the topic of divorce. In later chapters we will discuss how it is essential for your child to feel that any thought or feeling he has about the divorce is okay, as people cannot heal from trauma if they don't allow themselves to fully and openly experience their emotions.

I'm the Only One Trying to Communicate in a Healthy Way!

Sharon, 45, writes: "My husband and I have been separated for a little over a month now, and we have decided that we are moving toward divorce and not reconciliation. I am committed to making my kids' transition as easy as possible, but my husband doesn't have the kids' best interests in mind at all. He blames me for the separation in front of the kids, and God knows what he says when he's alone with them. I asked him to sit down with me and plan what to say when we finally tell them that we are getting a divorce, but he refuses to work with me. He also refused to read any articles I sent him on divorce, and laughed when I recommended this book, saying, 'Maybe you should have put this much effort into our marriage instead.' I am so angry, but worse, I am scared about the impact of his words and actions on my kids. What should I do?"

Dear Sharon, you are in a tough spot, and I empathize with you. If it is any consolation, this is a pretty common situation among couples engaged in conflictual divorces, which is the majority. It is rare that two sparring co-parents would accept advice or book recommendations from one another, no matter what is in the best interests of the kids, and even the best parent may act spiteful and self-absorbed in the face of the tremendous stressor of divorce.

Try to reframe this situation and to limit your expectations of your husband. Don't assume that he has the emotional resources to deal with the divorce in the same way that you are. After all, it seems like he would have chosen to remain together, despite your problems. Therefore, don't expect that he will be as prepared and committed to answering your children's questions and talking to them about the divorce in a healthy and adaptive way. If he is sad or angry, he may say things that you wish he wouldn't say, like blaming you or attacking your character.

If your husband continues to blame you for the divorce in front of the children, you must start to defend yourself, but only without attacking him in retaliation. Two wrongs don't make a right. If a child tells you, "Daddy says we're all in this situation because of you," you can respond, "My marriage to Daddy wasn't working out for many reasons. There is not one person that is to blame for a divorce. I am sorry for anything either Daddy or I did that led to the divorce, because it was hard for you." Read more about how to defend yourself in these cases in Chapter 7.

Other than continuing to tell your children that you are not solely to blame for the divorce, there is no way to make your husband act differently toward you or your children. Focus on reading this book and figuring out your own best way to communicate with your children. Try to avoid spending time and energy on wishing your husband would interact differently with you or your kids. As long as he continues to see your kids and to parent them well (although maybe not how you would parent them yourself), focus on your own relationship with your kids and not on how he communicates with them.

Key points from this chapter:

- Planning your initial divorce announcement can help the conversation go more smoothly

- It is helpful to think in advance about how you'll answer your children's common questions about divorce

- Emphasize that nobody is to blame for the divorce, not either parent alone, and certainly none of the kids

- Remember that your children crave stability and routine, and try to reassure them that you will keep things as predictable as possible

- Make your children feel that they were, and will always be, loved and wanted

- There are ways to change your language that will positively impact how your child views your divorce

- No matter how your co-parent communicates with your children, you can commit to communicating the healthiest way you know how

CHAPTER 3

THE CONFIDANTE PROBLEM

When you're going through a divorce, or any difficult period in your life, it is natural to want someone to listen to you and to provide love and comfort. Often, it seems like the person who best understands your problems and frustrations with your co-parent is the same person who has been watching these issues unfold—your child.

Children who are described as intelligent, "old souls," or "wise beyond their years" often fall into the trap of acting as a confidante or best friend to at least one of their parents. And of course, the reason that a child may appear precocious in this way is because he was bearing witness to his parents' conflictual marriage for many years. Additionally, daughters are more likely to act as a friend, confidante, and advisor to parents in emotional distress. Girls often act as caretakers with younger siblings, and are more naturally predisposed to take on this role with a suffering parent as well. Only or oldest children also are more susceptible to taking on the role of one parent's special friend. Oldest children are given more responsibilities than younger children, and only children often start out feeling that they are on a peer level with their parents. Sensitive children also often take on the confidante role, as they instinctively know how to comfort others, and are intuitive and perceptive.

A pattern of treating a child as a confidante is easy to fall into, but it can deeply damage your child. Children, even if they are mature or precocious, are still children. They are not developmentally able to handle adult issues and emotions, especially not the extreme emotions that arise within a divorce. Of course, all children want to be perceived as mature, responsible, and important, so they will hide from you any anxiety or stress that they feel when hearing you discuss issues that make them uncomfortable. This may make you think that your child is different from other children, and is able to understand and process adult issues and feelings and emerge unscathed. Some parents even believe that exposure to adult emotions and "real-life" problems will make a child stronger, or will teach her "the way the world really works."

EMOTIONAL BOUNDARIES

In a healthy parent-child relationship, a child's emotional boundaries get stronger as she ages. A baby has very few thoughts or feelings that aren't shared with a parent, via crying, smiling, pointing, or fussing. A preschooler keeps a lot more of his thoughts and feelings private, and a teenager is exponentially more private than that.

In contrast, parents' boundaries generally get more permeable as children age. With older children, parents share more of their thoughts and feelings. It would be ridiculous for a parent to tell a baby about household finances, and this would be confusing and possibly burdensome to an elementary-school-age child. But a parent can and should be able to discuss finances with a teenager to a greater extent, particularly as this may be relevant to plans for a job or college tuition.

However, there are certain areas that do not have any positive contribution to a child's wellbeing or knowledge about the world, and can only have a negative effect. Topics that breach normal parent-child boundaries and are not appropriate to discuss with children include:

- One parent's lack of financial contribution
- One parent's hurtful behavior toward the other
- Infidelity
- A parent's sex life

- Resentment toward a co-parent
- Anger toward a co-parent
- Anxiety about the future
- A co-parent being "wrong" about how to parent
- The early history of the marriage and when things started to go wrong
- A litany of every detailed event that transpired in the parents' attempt to save the marriage (for example, saying you went to counseling is fine, but not the focus of each session, the thoughts of the counselor, the false starts at reconciliation, and so forth)

A child may ask about these topics, even persistently. However, no matter who initiates conversations of this nature, they can be psychologically harmful to your child. If a child is an adult (and adulthood nowadays, culturally and psychologically, seems to commence after college), you can broach these topics at your discretion, but it is still not very emotionally generous to your child. There is no positive side to your child being saddled with your painful thoughts, memories, or fears.

ENMESHMENT

The term for a parent-child relationship that is excessively and unhealthily close is *enmeshed*. Enmeshed relationships are characterized by a lack of boundaries between a parent and a child. In an enmeshed relationship, the parent shares thoughts, feelings, hopes, and fears that are not developmentally appropriate for a child to hear. Children's greatest desire is to feel close to and loved by their parents, so if they intuit or are told that a parent needs emotional support, they want to provide it. They may even repeatedly ask the parent to confide, until it really seems like the child is the one that is creating the confidante relationship. Even if your child initiates conversations that involve adult-level confidences, it is your obligation to avoid or end these conversations. Your child may seem calm and understanding during your conversations, but she is likely ruminating about these ideas and exerting emotional energy figuring out how to solve your problems.

Child As Baby

Sometimes a parent keeps an enmeshed child in a "baby" role, where a growing child is not granted age-appropriate increases in independence or privileges. The parent unconsciously wants to keep the child from growing up and having his own life, which would necessitate leaving the parent. When one parent keeps a child in a baby role, conflict often ensues with the other parent, who views this as unhealthy. Additionally, the child himself may push back, either overtly with rebellion or covertly by sneaking around to do things that his peers are doing. On the other hand, some children feel comfortable in the baby role, and do not want to upset their parents by acting more mature. This leads to a different issue: These children remain "stuck" at a young emotional age, and have difficulties throughout their lives because of their inability to take on responsibilities and act in an age-appropriate way.

Child As Parent

Another type of enmeshment is *parentification*. In this dynamic, the parent and the child psychologically switch roles, with the child taking care of the emotional and even physical needs of his parent. This dynamic is observed frequently with children of depressed or alcoholic parents, in addition to parents struggling in the aftermath of divorce. The children are the ones who cook, clean, pay bills, call parents' workplaces to make excuses for absences, and accompany parents to appointments (which they have reminded the parents to attend). Parents in these dynamics often say things like, "What would I do without you?" or "Without you, I wouldn't be here." These messages of dependence reinforce the child's perception that he must take care of his parent or the parent would not be able to survive. This is a very heavy burden for a child, particularly one who is struggling with the dissolution and reshaping of his family post-divorce.

Child As Surrogate Partner

In a third form of enmeshment, a child acts as a "surrogate spouse" to an opposite-sex parent. I have witnessed this more frequently between boys and their mothers, possibly due to the fact that a greater percentage of children spend more time with their mothers after a divorce. When a mother and her son have an enmeshed bond, the son often is unable to have a positive relationship with his father. He has been told too many negative things about his dad, and identifies with and feels protective of his mother. In addition to sabotaging the relationship between the son and his father, an enmeshed mother-son bond can prevent both the mother and the son from developing healthy emotional relationships with real romantic partners in the future.

Long-Term Consequences of Enmeshment

Enmeshment in any form steals your child's childhood. Rather than filling their lives with healthy and outward-directed pursuits such as school, activities, socializing, and, later, romantic relationships, children who are enmeshed with their parents either spend excessive amounts of time with their parents or an excessive amount of emotional energy on worrying about their parents' needs.

Enmeshment has long-lasting and tragic consequences for children. Although adult children of enmeshed parents may desperately want to forge their own independent lives, they often feel trapped by a crushing feeling of guilt at the thought of "abandoning" the enmeshed parent by setting healthy boundaries. Thus, even in a child's own adulthood, he cannot be free of the burden of his parent's emotional needs. And when the adult child enters a long-term romantic relationship, the primary bond continues to be between the adult child and his own parent, rather than the adult child and his frustrated, lonely partner, which frequently sabotages these intimate relationships. One fictional example of enmeshment occurs in *Loverboy*, a novel by Victoria Redel.

END THE CONFIDANTE DYNAMIC

If you recognize any of your behavior in these descriptions, don't berate yourself, but also don't ignore the situation. You did not irreparably damage your child, but you now have the knowledge to change course.

Children are highly resilient and able to switch trajectories easily if gently guided in a better direction by an adult. This is why therapy works so well with kids. The best thing to do now is recognize that you have fallen into a dysfunctional pattern with your child, and take full responsibility to get your relationship onto a healthier track.

A good first step is to openly tell your child that you've been wrong to share so many of your feelings about the divorce and your child's other parent. You then apologize and tell the child what the new pattern will be going forward. Specifically, tell your child that you will no longer be sharing so many adult, private thoughts and feelings. Say that these feelings are only for adults, and it can be stressful for kids to hear about how upset their parents are all of the time. Most children know the word "inappropriate," so this is a good word to use to describe how you have been acting.

Your child may first protest, equating a loss of confidences with a loss of love or respect, so be sure to reassure your child that it is actually because you love her so much that you are making this healthy change. Explain that you have been relying too much on your child, and you don't want your child to worry about you anymore. Reassure your child that you will be fine, and that you will be turning to other adults and to professionals to help you with the stress of the divorce. Although your child may say that your confidences are welcome, she will eventually feel relieved if you stop sharing the details of your emotional life. This will free your child to be a child again.

NO MESSENGERS, SPIES, OR SECRETS

When parents feel overly close to their children, they often unintentionally put them in very difficult situations, by using the children as messengers, spies, or secret keepers. Adult children of divorce often complain bitterly about their parents having forced them to deliver, retrieve, or hide information. These situations force a child into a no-win situation in which any action he chooses leads to a parent possibly feeling angry, hurt, or betrayed.

It is very damaging for a child to act as a messenger between two loved parents. Not only do children often get these messages wrong, they feel extremely anxious about acting in this role. They correctly assume that their parents are too angry with one another to be able to communicate effectively, and this is very stressful for a child to contemplate. Children also understand the subtext of messages, which means that they understand that one parent is often judging the other's behavior.

If a child is asked to secretly get information, e.g., to look for evidence of a new partner staying overnight in a parent's home, this makes the child feel like a double agent. There is no way for him to win: Either he disappoints the parent who asked for the information, or he is duplicitous toward the parent on whom he is spying. It is also cruel to pump your child for information about your co-parent upon the child's return to your home, or to manipulate him into telling you information that your co-parent would not want you to know. This information can include intimate details of a new relationship, specifics of meals or activities that you can then use against your co-parent (e.g., by saying he does not feed your child healthy foods), or financial information about your co-parent. If a child realizes that he has unwittingly been duped into "telling on" his other parent, he will feel guilty, ashamed, and probably very angry and resentful toward you, particularly later in life.

Sometimes a parent will entreat a child not to tell a co-parent about something he has witnessed or experienced, e.g., that Mommy has a boyfriend, or that Dad bought a new car. This is just as unfair and anxiety-provoking as when a child is asked to spy. A child knows that omitting certain information would be perceived by his co-parent as lying, so this is asking your child to be dishonest and to treat one parent with more respect than he treats the other. Any situation where a child is explicitly asked to lie or withhold information from a parent, or to be more open with one parent than with another, is emotionally abusive. These no-win situations plunge children into serious psychological discomfort that is generally resolved by the child deciding to emotionally withdraw from one or both parents.

Here's an example of one way that asking a child to deliver a message can go awry. Jean, 43, asked her seven-year-old son, Jason, to tell his father about the nightmares he had been having on Sunday nights after returning home from his father's house. Jason correctly assumed that this was a way for his mother to tell his father that he was doing something wrong during his weekends with Jason. Jean was passive-aggressively using this message to underscore her point that the kids should be returned earlier on Sundays.

To protect his father and decrease conflict between his parents, Jason never told his father about his nightmares, and he also stopped telling his mother when he woke up from bad dreams. Not only did the message go undelivered, but the child's obvious psychological distress, manifesting itself in nightmares, was never addressed. Jason's father never had the opportunity to learn about the nightmares, and Jean thought that Jason's father ignored the message and she became even angrier with this latest "evidence" of his lack of concern about Jason's wellbeing. No solution was offered by either parent to help Jason with his nightmares or difficulty with the evening drop-offs. Had Jean called Jason's father herself and non-attackingly mentioned her concern about the nightmares, it is possible that Jason's father would have been worried enough to sit down with her and brainstorm solutions to this issue. Instead, indirect communication through the child led to the worst of all outcomes.

Another issue with using children as messengers is that, often, parents get distressed at the content of the message, and this is evidenced by their reaction. When a child delivers a message, he is often shocked when a parent's face changes, expressing sadness, anger, or derision, which the child interprets as directed at him instead of directed at the other parent. A child then feels duped by one parent into making the other parent angry with him. He feels betrayed and exposed, and is much less likely to communicate openly with either parent in the future, having seen that communication can easily turn into something inexplicably dangerous. This also teaches a child to be wary of communication within intimate relationships as an adult.

If you have been delivering or receiving messages or requests to or from your co-parent through your child, try to change this dynamic. Immediately contact your co-parent to schedule a face-to-face or phone meeting about the issue of using kids as messengers. Without blaming your co-parent, and with accepting responsibility for your part in this dynamic, explain that you're concerned about the effects on the child in the role of go-between.

During your meeting, try to come up with a way to communicate without involving your child. Emails and texts are preferred to phone calls, because each parent has a written record of what transpired, which can be referred to in terms of remembering times and dates, financial agreements, issues with the children, and other things that may come up. If you've previously been difficult to get ahold of, due to negative feelings that arise when you interact with your co-parent, admit this and commit to being more available for discussion in the future. This will help ensure that the children do not have to be involved in the communication process.

APPROPRIATE CONFIDANTES

It is essential to find yourself an adult confidante if you find yourself wanting to confide emotionally in your child. Sadly, many divorced people find themselves with a marked dearth of friends for various reasons. If your marriage was doing poorly for a while prior to the divorce, it's common to hunker down and feel depressed, without the motivation to go out and interact with others. You may have felt ashamed about your marital issues, which leads to limiting social activities and even phone calls out of a desire to keep your distress hidden. Sometimes after a divorce, one spouse ends up with most of the mutual friends, and the other is left without a social circle. No matter how lonely you feel, there are many venues in which to find adult interaction and support. Divorced individuals often end up with a whole new coterie of friends just a few years after a divorce, although they may feel lonely and isolated in the initial few months.

Friends and Family

Some lucky people have friends or family members who want to provide emotional support. Although you want to be sure not to excessively burden any of your friends and family members with consistent complaints about your divorce and your co-parent, you can certainly invite them out for coffee, ask them for babysitting if you are in a pinch, or call them when you're feeling lonely or sad.

Your divorced friends or family members will likely become closer to you as you go through your divorce. Many people who have been divorced for years want to help newly divorced people navigate their new lives by providing advice and emotional support. In contrast, your single or married friends and family members may not understand what you're going through, because they haven't been there themselves. This doesn't mean they don't want to listen and support you, but you may want to find someone who has been in your shoes or who has training to help you deal with your issues.

Therapists

A therapist is an excellent choice for a confidante, as you can get the emotional support you need in addition to learning coping skills and new ways of moving forward in your situation. Therapy is a very common and reasonable choice for newly divorced people. Many divorcees decide to use their divorce as a catalyst for changing their life, taking stock of how they feel now as well as who they want to be in the future. Therapy can help you figure out existential and identity-focused issues like these, as well as help you address the anxiety, depression, grief, and anger that accompany most divorces. Most therapists are very familiar with the issues facing divorced or soon-to-be-divorced clients, but don't hesitate to ask your prospective therapist about his or her experience with clients who are undergoing divorces. Also, use your first therapy session with any new therapist as a time to assess whether you think you would be a good fit with this provider. It may take a couple of tries to find a therapist you click with, but once you do, this relationship can be invaluable in helping you move past your divorce and figure out how to rebuild your life.

Groups and Classes

There are many support groups for divorced or separated individuals, like Parents Without Partners, DivorceCare, the National Divorce Support Alliance, or any divorce support group on Meetup.com in your area. Many individuals find these support groups to be a gold mine of potential friends (and even new romantic partners, if and when you feel ready to date). Of course, you don't have to find friends at groups geared only for divorced people. There are many social groups for singles on Meetup.com and other sites, and you can also find groups and classes at your local recreation center, library, or community college. Running or walking groups, gym classes, and water/snow sport groups are great for fitness-and-health-minded people. Find a group or a class where you have the greatest chance of making new friends with similar outlooks and values.

Online forums for divorced and separated people as well as forums for parents (single and partnered) can also be a source of virtual friends and confidantes. DivorcedMoms.com, SingleParentsNetwork.com, HuffPost Divorce, and the divorce forum on PsychCentral.com are just a few of the numerous online forums and resources for divorced people that welcome interaction and commentary. Although it is always nice to have a friend that you can talk to face-to-face, this just may not be feasible for many overwhelmed, busy, newly single parents. Moreover, many introverted people feel much more comfortable online than in real-life support groups. Online friendships are no less meaningful because they occur over the Internet rather than over dinner. Following the blogs of divorced parents could be another good way to find virtual support, and many bloggers are very receptive and responsive to comments and feedback. Since starting DrPsychMom.com I have been amazed at how friendly and tight-knit the blogging and online writing community can be, with many people telling me that they have online friends that they have never physically met that they consider to be closer friends than people they know in real life.

Even if you've never used your child as a confidante, it is still important to make friends and have a social life. Spending too much child-centered time does not allow your child to live his own life, nor does it model healthy adult behavior. Even if you're sharing custody and feel like you don't get enough time with your child, be sure to be conscious of both your child's need and your own need for alone time. Additionally, if you have no social life or hobbies, your child will feel very guilty when he's with his other parent, imagining you at home and lonely.

Key points from this chapter:

- Adult thoughts and feelings are for adults only

- Your child is not your confidante

- *Enmeshment*, or the lack of boundaries between parents and their children, can harm your child both now and in later life

- Do not use your child to transmit information openly or covertly between you and your co-parent

- If you find yourself relying on your child for emotional support, turn to an adult friend, a support group, or a therapist instead

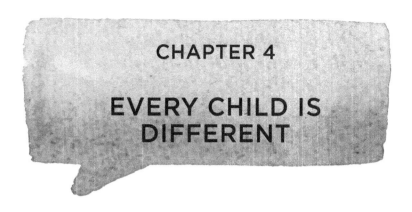

CHAPTER 4

EVERY CHILD IS DIFFERENT

There are many variables unique to your child that can affect his response to your divorce. Birth order, gender, and personality all can have distinct effects on how your child is likely to cope with divorce and the host of changes that accompany it. Although every child is different and some children are the exception to the rule, it is good to familiarize yourself with the most common ways that different types of children respond to divorce.

GENDER

If you have both sons and daughters, you may have already noticed many innate differences between them. For instance, boys typically externalize their negative feelings by "acting out." Conduct problems and social adjustment are worse for boys from divorced families than for girls. Girls more often internalize their negative feelings, and try to "be good" and behave in a way that will make a parent's life easier. They are likelier to fall into the confidante or caretaker role discussed in Chapter 3. Girls are more sensitive and observant regarding interpersonal relationships, as well. In *The Unexpected Legacy of Divorce*, the authors write that older girls often become more promiscuous after their parents' divorce, particularly if the daughters are in an environment where they see a lot more sex and physical affection than they saw previously (see Chapter 13).

Girls also fill a caretaker role more often than boys do, and become tangled in enmeshed relationships with at least one parent (see Chapter 3). They worry about younger siblings as though the older girls are "little mothers," which can lead to adoration or resentment from younger siblings, depending on their personalities and ages. See the vignette that follows for an example of how this dynamic can go awry.

My Daughter Is Trying to Be the Mom

Kyla, 45, writes: "My 10-year-old daughter and my 8-year-old son used to be close, but since my husband and I separated three months ago, they have been squabbling much more. My son has been more difficult, and my daughter gets angry with him, calling him a baby. She acts like she is his mother, telling him to clean up and get dressed. She even says 'Mommy has better things to do than yell at you!' My son yells, 'You're not Mom,' and then acts even worse out of spite. How do I fix this?"

———————————

Dear Kyla, you're right, it is important to deal with your children's fighting before their relationship is seriously damaged. Your son is struggling with the separation and acting out in predictable ways for his age. Your daughter, being an oldest child, identifies with you, and has taken on the role of a parent. It upsets her when her brother misbehaves, because she thinks it gives you added stress, and she wants to act as a second parent and share the burden of parenting with you now that you're alone.

Your daughter believes that her role has changed since the divorce. She may still yearn to be treated like a child but thinks that she needs to step up and become a second parent in this crisis situation. It sounds like she may be copying phrases that she has overheard, so you need to think about how you've been talking to your kids when you've been feeling stressed. If you've been conveying that you're stressed to your breaking point and always have more important things to do than deal with your kids' misbehavior, this is understandable, but this way of communicating is frightening your daughter. She is taking you literally and assuming that she needs to take some stress off your plate.

Tell your daughter that you think that she may be worried about you and that she is trying to help you by acting like a mom to her brother. Express that you appreciate her concern, but reassure her that you are able to parent both her and her brother without help. Apologize for any times that you may have said or implied that you were too stressed to deal with your kids, and reassure your daughter that you will always be there for her and her brother, even if you're feeling sad or stressed.

Since your daughter wants to help, make sure she has age-appropriate chores that she can do that can help you around the house. A child this age can prepare an easy dinner (sandwiches, salads) for the family, do laundry, care for pets, rake leaves, and so forth. This can make your daughter feel that she is helping out without having to act as a parent to her brother and thereby strain their relationship.

BIRTH ORDER

Each of your children will have a unique response to the divorce based in part on their place in the family. The effects of birth order are more salient the closer children are in age. When age differences between children are around seven years or greater, they may behave as two only children, while children only a year apart will have the strongest birth order effects. Let's explore how firstborns, middles, and youngest children each may prototypically respond to divorce. These are only guidelines; your individual child may not adhere entirely to these descriptions.

Oldest Children

Oldest children are used to being in charge. They are often more reliable and responsible than their siblings, and are more invested in following rules and making up rules for others to follow. Due to their preoccupation with following the rules, oldest children are likelier to think of one parent as "right" and one parent as "wrong," especially if infidelity, violence, or addiction led to your divorce.

Parents often rely on oldest children for childcare, help around the house, and to generally be "good" and free the parent to deal with younger children or household issues. This makes the oldest child particularly susceptible to falling into the "confidante" pattern discussed in Chapter 3. Parents must be conscious of ensuring that their oldest children do not feel that they must take care of the emotional and physical needs of other family members. Oldest children need as much love and reassurance as other children in the family, but they often get less because their parents treat them more like little adults. More is expected of them and less warmth and nurturance often comes their way.

Oldest children who are given many more responsibilities after a divorce may resent both their parents and their siblings. As adults, they may feel that the divorce not only robbed them of a two-parent home but also took away their childhood, replacing it with obligations like caring for younger siblings and emotionally distraught parents. It is therefore essential to remember not to overburden your oldest child with too many requests for support. Certainly, children should all chip in, but be careful that you do not give the oldest child all of the new responsibilities that come with divorce (watching younger siblings, packing each week, remembering schedule changes, and so forth).

Also, be sure that you allow your oldest child to openly express her feelings about the divorce. We will read in Chapter 5 about the importance of expressing negative emotions if we want these emotions to lose their intensity. Oldest children often pride themselves on acting like adults, and they may squelch their feelings in order to seem more mature to you and to their siblings. It is easy for overwhelmed parents to feel relieved that that there is one fewer openly upset child to deal with, and not probe too deeply into the oldest child's feelings. But try not to just breathe a sigh of relief that your oldest child is coping so well, and certainly don't praise her for this. As we will learn in Chapter 5, this would likely stop your child from approaching you with negative feelings that she may have under the surface.

Middle Children

Middle children often get lost in the shuffle despite their parents' best intentions. When they were born, their older siblings likely took priority, and then they were ousted from the baby role a few years later. To deal with their insecurity about being neither the oldest nor the youngest, these children usually try to figure out a specific identity that helps them claim a place in the family, like "the joker" or "the dramatic one." Despite their lower self-esteem, middle children can often be more socially adept than their siblings, as they have had to figure out how to fit in and how to get others to pay attention to them. They are excellent team players and collaborators, since they are used to dealing with an oldest sibling who usually gets her way. Since middle children are good at making connections, their peer relationships are very important to them. These friendships can even be a second family for a child who does not feel that he has a special place in his own family. Therefore, parents should try to ensure that all children, but especially the middle child, continue to have visits with friends even amidst the tumult of a divorce.

Middle children are also skilled manipulators but use their social skills to make peace and avoid conflict, according to *The Secret Power of Middle Children: How Middleborns Can Harness Their Unexpected and Remarkable Abilities* by Catherine Salmon, PhD, and Katrin Schumann. Thus it is critical that you do not take middle children at face value when they say that they are fine, and when they seem to be coping perfectly with your divorce. Take the time to really sit down with your middle child and talk about his feelings. Middle children don't often get one-on-one time, so it would be a great idea to set aside special weekly time just for you and your middle child to talk and do fun activities, like the ones listed in Chapter 14. Extra attention is important for all kids going through their parents' divorce but especially for middle children, who often feel ignored or neglected.

Youngest Children

Youngest children have been babied by both their parents and their siblings throughout their lives. While this treatment makes them feel cherished and loved, they also yearn to be seen as impressive, since they are always too little to do what the older children are doing. Since youngest children are usually protected from negative consequences of their behavior, they can feel invulnerable and turn into risk-takers.

As Jill Jones-Soderman and Allison Quattrocchi write in *How to Talk to Your Children about Divorce*, it is critical to watch out for youngest children during a divorce. As parents have increased demands on their time and emotional and physical energy, the "baby" may feel that he is expected to grow up instantly. Additionally, the youngest child may resent his siblings, who got to spend more time in the pre-divorce family, especially if family life was relatively stable prior to the divorce. Youngest children often worry that there won't be enough resources remaining for them after the divorce, whether this is college money or time with parents. There is a danger of them becoming envious of older siblings, which can hurt the sibling relationship right at the time that this relationship needs to be strongest.

To help your youngest child thrive during and after your divorce, it is important to reassure him that he will always be your baby, and that you still love him as much as you ever did. If he needs to take on new responsibilities, or face new realities, such as spending more time alone, stopping an activity that he enjoys, or getting a part-time job, do not expect him to immediately acclimate to these changes. Use empathy and validation, and do not tell your child that he is being self-centered or that he's "going to have to grow up." Don't let siblings speak to him this way either. Keep in mind that most parents coddle their youngest, so your own parenting likely shaped any self-centeredness that you see. If you want your youngest child to act more mature, give him concrete ways that he can help the family, and express your appreciation and gratitude when he rises to the occasion.

Only Children

Divorce may be particularly difficult for only children. This is true for children without any siblings as well as virtual only children, those who are separated by seven or more years from their closest sibling. Children with special-needs siblings can also feel like only children, particularly if the sibling is unable to engage interpersonally.

Only children are often high-achieving in school and extracurriculars, having had the benefit of all of their parents' focus and resources. These kids usually feel that they are the most important thing in their parents' lives, so it is unlikely that you will have to worry about your only child feeling lost in the shuffle and ignored during or after your divorce. This is a positive, but with this positive can come some negatives.

Only children generally feel a great sense of pressure to be "good" and to make their parents proud and happy. They have no siblings with whom to split this burden. Therefore, it is likely that your child is at risk of feeling that you and your co-parent are fighting over her attention, and that she is caught in the middle. This can make an only child feel highly conflicted and anxious, especially since these kids are typically more sensitive and conflict averse than children with siblings, due to a lack of exposure to sibling squabbling while growing up.

Only children are also at risk of feeling highly isolated after a divorce. They have no siblings with whom to discuss the divorce or associated life changes, and if they have to change neighborhoods or schools, it will be harder for a lone child to approach new potential friends or neighborhood kids than it would be for a pair or trio of siblings to do so. In new schools, siblings will be in different classes, but they still know that their sibling is a "new kid," too, which can be comforting. In contrast, only children often feel exposed and alone in social situations, particularly those that are new or intimidating.

Only children are at particular risk of becoming a parent's confidante, as discussed in Chapter 3. They are often verbally advanced and considered "precocious," because they spend a lot of one-on-one time with adults while growing up. This can make a parent incorrectly assume that only children are able to hear and deal with adult feelings, and even that these children can offer valuable advice. A child should never be put in the position of a "friend" or a confidante to a troubled parent. This is unfair and does not respect the child's need for boundaries.

When parenting an only child post-divorce, try to keep multiple points in mind. First, make sure your child spends lots of time with other children outside of school. As a single parent, everyone will advise you to spend quality time with your child, and this is certainly essential. But once your child turns three or four, a parent is no substitute for other children, and your child will still long for peer interaction. Therefore, at least once during the week and once on the weekend, your child should be interacting with other kids at activities or playdates.

Offer to bring friends along to special parent-child activities, too. One child and one parent does not usually make for a fun time at an amusement park, a magic show, a petting zoo, or a circus. Your child may be too self-conscious with just you there to enjoy the experience fully. It does not take away from your quality time with your child to include a friend; in fact, it will likely enhance the fun.

Pets can also be important "friends" for the only child of divorce. Often kids consider the pet to be a best friend and constant companion, and even a surrogate sibling. The best choice is a pet that can also serve as a conversation starter with other kids, like a friendly dog that can be walked. This pet could even move between both parents' homes with your child.

Remember not to treat your only child as a confidante, as we discussed in Chapter 3. Many only children are verbally advanced, from being around adults giving them undivided attention and talking to them on a more adult level. Don't mistake this verbal precocity for a child being more mature than she really is. Don't confide in your child about anything adult or divorce-related.

Lastly, make sure your only child knows you love her for who she is. Kids with siblings understand that their parents value different things about each child, and see that their parents respond appreciatively to their sense of humor, and to their sister's kindness, and to their brother's adventurousness. An only child knows that you love her, but she is the only game in town, so it may seem like you "have to" love her. This is exacerbated by divorce, because from the child's perspective, you really have nobody else to love now at all. Make sure you say you love your child's own specific qualities and that you're happy that you ended up with exactly the child that she is.

PERSONALITY

A great deal of research has been done on different personality styles in children, and how temperament affects responses to stressful situations. It is nearly impossible to change your child's innate personality and make him more easygoing and flexible, or more industrious and focused. It is essential that you respect the way your child is wired, because constantly trying to change him is going to stress your relationship to the breaking point.

Strong-Willed Children

Strong-willed children are often called "difficult," since they do not "go with the flow" but want their own way in everything. They are persistent and become focused on an idea or an activity to the exclusion of all else. This child has a tantrum when he does not get his way, and is very hard to soothe. He is frustrating to deal with for even the most patient parent, but it can be easier if you realize that your child is just wired this way and is not trying to be difficult.

Strong-willed children have particular difficulty coping with divorce. They want what they want when they want it, and if that is Mommy when they are at Daddy's house, or if it is to be hanging out with their friends on a weekend instead of spending time with a parent, they will be very upset. This child also has difficulty adapting to new routines or being flexible about living arrangements or schedules.

Parents of strong-willed children need to make a particular effort to give their children a voice in decisions that involve them. If a child is set on spending time with friends, for example, try to make this happen rather than insisting on time spent with you just because it's "your time." Trying to enforce strict rules with a strong-willed teenager is particularly unlikely to end well. This is a child who needs empathy, compromises, and to feel that he has a say in his own life. If you keep this in mind, your interactions may improve.

Children with Attention Deficit Hyperactivity Disorder (ADHD)

Parents of kids with ADHD have higher rates of divorce, as shown in a 2008 study conducted by doctors Brian T. Wymbs and William E. Pelham Jr. of SUNY Buffalo. The stress of parenting ADHD kids is hard on marriage, and it's therefore likely that divorced parents of kids with ADHD struggle more with co-parenting than do parents of non-ADHD kids. Children with ADHD pose many more challenges than other children, and parenting them can be overwhelming and demoralizing. The unpredictable behavior of an ADHD child can make parents feel like they are not in control of their own lives.

Another issue is that ADHD is highly heritable, and either one or both parents of ADHD kids are likely to have ADHD themselves, whether or not it has been formally diagnosed. Therefore, the difficulties that an ADHD child experiences in time management, organization, and remembering rules or assignments can be compounded by at least one parent's difficulty with the same issues. An ADHD child with an ADHD parent is a lot less likely to remember to take his medication, to show up on time to classes, and to make scheduled therapy or doctors' appointments. This parent will also struggle with teaching a child organization and time management skills that the parent does not possess. These issues get even worse when an ADHD parent is under stress from a divorce. (If you feel that a spouse's irresponsibility precipitated or exacerbated issues that led to your divorce, *The ADHD Effect on Marriage: Understand and Rebuild Your Relationship in Six Steps* by Melissa Orlov is an eye-opening book that may provide new insight into your prior marital issues and current co-parenting issues.)

The stress of a divorce can aggravate the everyday behavioral issues that characterize life with an ADHD child. If a child is unable to remember his backpack when it hangs on the same hook every day, and when his parent reminds him daily, he will forget it a lot more often when it is in a different place half the time and if his parent is too stressed to remember to remind him to take it. Furthermore, kids with ADHD are often very impulsive, and may act out more than other kids when they are feeling stressed or anxious, as they are during and after a divorce. These behaviors make parents angry and frustrated, and less likely to provide the positive affirmations and support that ADHD children need.

Kids with ADHD have an especially poor time adjusting to changes in routine, so it is important that parents try to make the schedule as consistent and predictable as possible. Also, children with ADHD find it particularly hard to self-motivate and do homework and chores without the guidance of an adult. Therefore, if a parent's work hours increase post-divorce, an ADHD preteen or teenager would likely do better in a structured afterschool or sports program than alone at home. If a child needs to be home alone, a parent should attempt to check in multiple times to remind the child that schoolwork needs to be done, to eat a snack, lock the door, and so forth.

Set your ADHD child up to succeed. See if you and your co-parent can have two sets of school supplies, one in each home. Buy doubles of anything that you can, like a special toy for nighttime, or even medications, glasses, or a retainer. Since ADHD is worse when kids are tired, see if you can avoid nighttime drop-offs where a stressful or stimulating transition can make a child less able to settle down to sleep. Instead, try having one co-parent drop the child at school and the other pick up the child that afternoon.

Many kids with ADHD also have Oppositional Defiant Disorder, a behavior pattern of having tantrums, being defiant, and being angry with parents and other authority figures. If you find your ADHD child's behavior worsening a great deal after the divorce, consider starting family therapy to get your relationship back on track.

Highly Sensitive Children

High sensitivity is a temperamental trait that is usually passed down from one or both parents. If your child is highly observant, perceptive, responsive to art and music, doesn't like loud or crowded places, and has difficulty "going with the flow," it is likely he is Highly Sensitive. This child experiences everything in life a hundred times more intensely than the average child. Highly Sensitive Children have many positive traits, such as creativity and profound empathy for others. They also are physically sensitive, and are harder hit by fatigue, illness, hunger, and changes of routine than the average child. They often vehemently dislike certain textures, odors, and sounds, making it frustrating to feed them or get them dressed. Older Highly Sensitive Children will ruminate more about peer interactions and may be more anxious about school and their social life.

Highly Sensitive Children are more likely to fall into the confidante role discussed in Chapter 3, because they are so attuned to their parents' emotions. Thus it is especially important to realize that your Highly Sensitive Child is not a small adult, no matter how perceptive and emotionally aware he may be. It is essential to make a special effort to shield Highly Sensitive Children from conflict and intense parental emotions whenever possible, because they will notice and brood about any negativity that they see.

Highly Sensitive Children often find it very difficult to accept that they will miss one parent when spending time with the other, which means that open communication between co-parents is essential. It is not a failure if your child still misses her other parent during her weekend with you; instead, you can take this as comforting evidence of your child's healthy relationship with your co-parent. With all children, but especially Highly Sensitive Children, phone calls may be helpful in allowing your child to maintain connection with one parent during her time with the other.

Highly Sensitive Children also need particular care when introducing a new partner into the mix. As we discuss in Chapter 12, meeting a parent's new partner can be a delicate and difficult situation. Highly Sensitive Children will easily sense if they are no longer a parent's priority, and have been replaced by a parent's new partner, or even their parent's partner's kids. They will ruminate about this displacement, whether it is real or perceived, and will be sensitive to even the most subtle changes in your behavior or attitude toward them.

If you are also Highly Sensitive, you may be able to understand your child better than his other parent does, but you are also more sensitive yourself, so you may find it harder to deal with the emotional demands that this child places upon you. If you are not Highly Sensitive but are parenting a Highly Sensitive Child, this can be very frustrating, as you genuinely don't understand why everything is such a "big deal." Parents of Highly Sensitive Children need to use empathy (see Chapter 6) even more frequently than other parents, because it can be extremely difficult to understand why your child is experiencing such intense emotions regularly. Read *The Highly Sensitive Child: Helping Our Children Thrive When the World Overwhelms Them* by Elaine N. Aron to better understand your child and how he is wired.

Children with Medical or Psychological Issues

Children who have many doctor's or therapist's appointments, or who are frequently ill, may also deal particularly poorly with divorce. Parents have other issues on their minds, and this child's appointments, medication management, and general care may fall through the cracks. Children with depression, anxiety, or an eating disorder will likely find that a divorce exacerbates these issues, as any uncertainty or significant routine change makes psychological issues flare up. Further, children with stomach issues, eczema, migraines, and all manner of physical ailments are very sensitive to stress.

Children with special needs, like developmental delays, sensory issues, or children on the autism spectrum, are especially hard-hit by changes in routine, and are less able to understand why a divorce happened. These kids may be more confused by divorce and less able to readily perceive a link between parents' unhappiness in a marriage and the current divorce. Kids whose developmental age is much younger than their chronological age can run into issues when they are expected to react in new ways that are beyond their capability, such as being flexible about living or sleeping arrangements, or acclimating to not seeing both parents as frequently as they used to.

With all of these children, there are logistical issues that have to be managed as part of the co-parenting plan. Appointments with therapists and doctors and special schools or tutors all require time and/or money, and parents can become particularly upset with one another if each feels that the other is not committed to the child's care. Co-parents likely both value necessary treatment for a child, but sometimes they do not agree on the definition of "necessary." If you and your co-parent do not agree on what treatment or services are needed, you must hash this out where your child cannot witness it, possibly with the aid of a counselor and/or mediator.

Many children feel guilty that their issues cause extra strife and stress for their parents, and this is multiplied greatly in a high-conflict divorce. Sometimes children will pretend that they are feeling better just so their parents don't have to fight with each other over what treatment is needed, deal with the stresses of getting them to and from their appointments, and worry about financial and insurance-related issues. To protect against this, commit to keeping your child's medical or psychological treatment consistent at least through the divorce and for a year afterward. If your child says that she no longer needs treatment, firmly and kindly say that divorce is a difficult time and it is important to you that she continues to have extra support. Even if your child is really doing better, having more attentive, caretaking adults in her life is always positive, particularly during a divorce.

EQUAL TREATMENT FOR SIBLINGS

When one child is younger or more vulnerable, or requires special care and vigilance, it is common for siblings to get short shrift. Don't focus solely on helping your more overtly vulnerable child while you assume that your other, "easier" child will be just fine. Even if this child appears to be coping excellently, he may also be hiding his difficulties because he believes that his role is to not burden his parents even more than they already are. It is common for older children in a family, or children who are "easier," to resent their siblings for always being prioritized by Mom and Dad.

Another common issue is that siblings of a vulnerable child become replacement caregivers for this child when parents are stressed or occupied. The same sort of sensitive, empathic child that becomes a confidante for a troubled parent can easily become a stand-in parent for a sibling in distress. While it is wonderful for siblings to be a source of comfort and solace to one another, this isn't always the outcome of a caretaking relationship. In fact, one of the most common reasons for sibling estrangement is that an older sibling resents having been forced to care for a younger one. See "I Hated My Brother" in Chapter 1 to see how this situation can result in a damaged sibling relationship.

Your children's sibling relationship needs to be a paramount priority. Remember, sibling relationships will likely be the longest relationships of your children's lives. In any situation where someone will end up being the "bad guy," make sure it is you and not one sibling. For example, if your oldest child can't take dance lessons because you need the money for your younger child's tutor, don't say this aloud. Instead, say that you just can't afford the lessons. Also, try to give equal time to each child, and equal amounts of fun one-on-one activities, even if one child asks for these and the other does not.

Key points from this chapter:

- Unique traits and circumstances affect your child's reaction to a divorce

- Saddling children with many new responsibilities and roles can lead to adverse outcomes

- Vulnerable children must have their routines kept as stable as possible

- Siblings must be treated fairly and their relationship should be a priority

CHAPTER 5

HOW EMOTIONS WORK

Most people are unaware of the science behind emotions, although they certainly know when they feel good or bad. It is important to know how emotions work, so that you can be sure to provide your child with space to express himself, clarify and process his feelings, and move past the negative feelings that arise from your divorce. Even the most amicable divorce, or, conversely, a divorce that ends a terribly conflictual marriage, will lead to a sense of loss in most children.

With the dissolution of the marriage comes the loss of your child's cherished fantasy that things will magically change and he will find himself in a happy, non-divorced family in the future. This loss can be expressed as sadness, anger, resentment, and grief. Furthermore, your child will likely feel a great deal of anxiety about his changing circumstances. Even if your child does not express any of these feelings openly, at least some of them will be felt on a deep internal level. The way that your child interprets and processes his feelings at this critical stage will affect how he views family, relationships, trust, and intimacy in later life.

It is also important to be aware of your own emotions throughout your divorce. Divorce leads to many intense feelings, both positive and negative. These emotions wash over you in waves, starting with initial sadness and anger when you realize you'll be divorcing, and continuing with feelings of grief and loss even years after your divorce is final. Resentment and jealousy are other common emotions that arise during the divorce process. Emotions during divorce can be intense, contradictory, and surprising. This can be seen by the startling fact, divulged in therapists' offices, that many highly conflictual divorcing couples still have sex. This certainly indicates that emotions can run high and lead people to do seemingly irrational things during the upheaval of divorce.

It is unhealthy to deny or minimize your feelings, even if they are painful or confusing. Understanding and accepting your own emotions will enable you to cope more effectively with the trauma and stress of divorce. This self-awareness and self-compassion will also better position you to guide your child through his own difficult and overwhelming feelings.

TYPES OF EMOTIONS

In *Emotion in Psychotherapy*, Leslie S. Greenberg and Jeremy D. Safran distinguish between primary emotions and secondary emotions. It is important to know the difference between these two types of emotions in order to better understand how and why you and your child feel the way that you do.

Primary Emotions

Primary emotions include "happiness," "sadness," "anger," and "fear." These emotions are normal and healthy sources of information about the world around us, that occur in response to external events. If someone cuts you off in traffic, you feel angry. This makes perfect sense: Your rights were violated, and you were put in a potentially dangerous situation. The evolutionary basis of anger is to bring a person's attention to his rights being infringed upon, and to mobilize the person to defend himself against an attack. Sadness is another primary emotion, which indicates that a person has experienced loss. Fear indicates that there is danger nearby, and mobilizes a fight-or-flight response.

Primary emotions are short-lived, lasting only minutes or hours. An exception is sadness, which can last more than a day, according to *The*

Subtlety of Emotions by Aaron Ben Ze-'ev. One real-world example of how short-lived emotions can be is the fear you may have experienced when your car skids while driving. This fear only lasts for a couple of moments. However, if primary emotions are really so short-lived, you may be wondering why people often feel sad or angry for much longer than a few hours. In these cases, these people are feeling secondary emotions, not primary emotions.

Secondary Emotions

Primary emotions are natural responses to the environment, but secondary emotions involve a negative thought about oneself. If you are cut off in traffic, your primary emotion may be anger over having your rights violated. However, you may also experience shame, thinking that there must be something about you that makes others think they can cut you off. You may also feel guilty about getting angry, thinking that you have too quick of a temper. The anger will be fleeting, but the secondary emotions of shame and guilt will last, and will contribute to low self-esteem.

When people are taught, in their childhood or by society, that emotions are "bad," they begin to feel scared and ashamed of their emotions. This can lead to secondary emotions that continue to plague them for a lifetime. For example, if you feel anxious about social interactions, you then also begin to feel depressed over being the type of person who would get anxious in social interactions. Allowing yourself to openly express your primary emotions, and accept that they are normal and healthy, can help you avoid getting stuck in cycles of rumination, guilt, and shame.

Self-compassion and acceptance are very important in stopping the cycle of feeling ashamed of your natural emotions. This means that you need to show the same compassion and empathy for yourself as you would for anyone else that you love, like your child. When something bad happens to you, give yourself a break and treat yourself with love and understanding. Accept your emotions and tell yourself that they are natural, instead of beating yourself up for being weak, vulnerable, or otherwise shameful. Then your primary emotions can dissipate quickly, and won't turn into secondary emotions and linger.

SUPPRESSING EMOTIONS DOESN'T WORK

Let's try a thought experiment now. Okay . . . Now, whatever you do, don't think of a white bear!

What did you think of? Probably a white bear. Paradoxically, trying to force your mind to not think of a white bear actually focuses your mind more completely on this image. The same thing happens with negative emotions. If you tell your child, "Don't be sad," she might be able to force the sadness out of consciousness in that moment, but it will likely pop up somewhere else, like an emotional game of Whack-a-Mole. Your child's sadness may manifest itself in nightmares, irritability, or depression. Teaching your child that it's okay to feel sad, angry, or anxious is ironically the best way to help her deal with these emotions, and these emotions will pass more quickly if they are acknowledged and accepted.

So many of our struggles are due to judging ourselves for our emotions and finding fault with ourselves. The most helpful strategy for dealing with negative emotions is the simplest—accept them.

Maria and Emotional Suppression

Maria is a 44-year-old newly divorced mom. Her husband cheated on her and left her with three kids under the age of twelve. Maria prides herself on staying in control at all times. Her mother was a single mom struggling to pay the bills, and Maria was her oldest child. She looked to Maria for comfort and companionship, and Maria learned that having any negative emotions would make her mother very upset. She would tell Maria that anger is "bad" and that good girls don't get angry.

Now, although Maria feels betrayed, angry, and resentful in the wake of her divorce, she does not allow herself to express these emotions, even to herself. When friends ask if she is angry or bitter about her situation, she says, "I'm fine. What would be the point of being angry when it's over and done with?" By continuing to push down her anger, Maria is ensuring that it will just keep popping back up. Her natural emotion of anger never gets a chance to live its full life cycle of increase, peak, and then decrease. Her anger continues to pop up in behaviors like eating too much, snapping at her kids, and not being able to focus at work.

Maria should definitely not express her anger to her kids, but expressing it openly to her friends, family members, or a therapist would likely help her process it and move forward. Even openly expressing her anger to herself, by writing about it or even just talking about it in her own head would be helpful, and would allow her to let these emotions out and then move on.

THE LIFE CYCLE OF EMOTIONS

As we have discussed, primary emotions are relatively short-lived. Also, an emotion does not maintain the same intensity over its lifespan. Instead, the life of an emotion is shaped like a bell curve, with a natural peak and decrease. Many people fear that painful emotions, if not stopped, will continue to escalate continuously. Others fear that painful emotions will continue at a steady intensity, forever, like a straight, steady line.

These ideas stem from the fact that when people experience overwhelming negative emotions, they try to escape from or suppress the emotions. They have only experienced the emotion's rise in intensity, because they don't sit with the emotion long enough to experience its natural decrease over time. Therefore, people in the throes of an intense emotion doubt that any such decrease will ever occur, and so they try to avoid, suppress, or escape negative emotions in the first place. Counterintuitively, though, the only way to get over negative emotions is to allow yourself to fully experience them as they peak and inevitably decrease.

Let's say you're scared of public speaking and your boss asks you to give a presentation. You believe that your fear will be intolerable and you won't be able to do it. You will likely make an excuse and get out of doing the presentation (avoidance), or say "I'm not scared, I'm not scared," and race through the presentation, barely aware of what you are saying (suppression), or you might even take a Xanax before the presentation (escape).

None of these common coping mechanisms allows you to see that, a few minutes into the presentation, your fear would naturally peak and decrease, and you would survive. You would likely also feel relieved and proud of yourself, and thus your brain would make new connections between public speaking and positive emotions. You may even have done a great job once you hit your stride. Instead, since you avoided, suppressed, or escaped from your anxiety, you continue to think, "I could never enjoy or succeed at public speaking." Even in the scenario where you raced through the presentation, you continue to feel anxious about public speaking, because you suppressed your anxiety rather than allowing yourself to fully experience its peak and decrease. You will remain scared that next time you won't be able to power through.

INVALIDATING YOUR CHILD'S EMOTIONS

Invalidation is when you tell someone that his or her feelings are not valid—or that they are wrong. It is difficult to experience, or to see your child experience, negative emotions such as anxiety, fear, sadness, and anger. Therefore, we often make the mistake of calling these "bad" emotions, and try to prevent ourselves and our children from experiencing them. For example, we say things like, "That's nothing to get upset about!" or "Don't be mad; he didn't mean it." These remarks are well-intentioned but very invalidating. They make people feel that their emotions are "wrong" or "bad," and should be suppressed or avoided. Unfortunately, there is no magic pill that eliminates all painful emotions. If they are avoided or suppressed, they will actually be experienced with greater intensity, or will manifest themselves in another form.

Additionally, when you see your child upset about something that you think is "not worth" getting upset about, it is natural to try and challenge your child's thoughts and feelings. Unfortunately, emotions cannot be argued away. When you tell your child, "That's not worth getting mad about," you're invalidating his emotional experience, which will make him even more distraught. You're also being illogical, because feelings are not "right" or "wrong"; they are natural sources of information about the environment.

All psychological disorders and emotional problems are worsened by invalidation. This is because pain, when minimized or denied, can never heal. Invalidation sabotages marriages and other interpersonal relationships. Alcoholic and other dysfunctional families thrive on invalidation, as children are not allowed to acknowledge that a parent is drunk and out of control. Instead, everyone pretends that a flagrantly dysfunctional behavior is not occurring at all, which is crazy-making for a child (and everyone else).

Invalidation is also a hallmark of emotional, physical, and sexual abuse. In these situations, an abuser tells the child that her normal feelings of discomfort, pain, or fear are not real, or are wrong. The child is repeatedly hurt, without any recognition or acknowledgment of her pain. As mentioned previously, invalidation is "crazy-making," and it is also at the root of gaslighting, where victims' feelings are purposely denied or manipulated in order to make them question their sanity. This term is used in the 1944 Ingrid Bergman film *Gaslight*, in which a husband purposefully drives his wife insane by flickering lights, making noises in the attic, and then claiming the very real experience was all in her head. Invalidation also occurs within parental alienation (see Chapter 7), where a child's natural love for his parent is denied and minimized, and the child therefore begins to doubt his own emotions.

Children who are invalidated never get a chance to learn that their emotions are natural and normal. They feel diminished, and assume that they are deficient compared to other people. Even worse, because their emotions are minimized or denied, they never learn effective strategies to deal with these emotions. Instead, they attempt to escape, suppress, or avoid them. As we have discussed, these coping strategies do not allow children to see that even their most painful emotions can be survived, and will peak and decrease. Invalidated children do not learn to accept their feelings and treat themselves with love and compassion. We will talk more about the importance of validation in the next chapter.

Let's take the example of Mira, age six, who was just told that she will get picked up by her dad on Thursdays after dance class from now on. She says to her mother, Elaine, "I don't want Daddy to get me! You won't know what I did in class and I won't be able to remember to show you later." Elaine is feeling guilty, as well as irritated. She thinks, "Nothing is ever easy." She says, "Come on, that's nothing to be upset about. How about you call me that night and tell me about dance class instead?" On the surface, this looks like a great way to solve this problem, and Mira may in fact stop complaining. However, Mira has also learned the following lessons:

- Expressing my feelings is not okay.
- My sadness and anger were "nothing," so it is silly to feel that way.
- It is not normal or acceptable to be disappointed or upset.
- Getting upset makes Mom's life more difficult.
- I better not feel that way anymore, so I should stop feeling upset or pretend I'm okay.

Now in addition to feeling sad that her mother won't be there to see her after dance class, Mira also feels guilty for making a problem, stupid for not thinking about other solutions, and silly or babyish for getting upset over "nothing." The likelihood of her feeling sad about disappointments in the future has not decreased, but the likelihood of her confiding in her mother about her sadness, either about this or any other issue, has decreased. Over time, she may also learn to escape, avoid, or suppress her sadness, or any other feeling that she is taught is unacceptable. She may do this with distraction, by acting out, or by compulsive or addictive behaviors as she gets older. We'll get back to Mira in our next section.

ACCEPTING, NOT AVOIDING, EMOTIONS

Acceptance and Commitment Therapy: An Experiential Approach to Behavior Change by Steven C. Hayes, Kirk D. Strosahl, and Kelly G. Wilson is centered around the idea of accepting feelings rather than trying to stop or challenge them. The theory is based on the idea that painful feelings are like quicksand—the more you try to escape from them, the deeper you find yourself stuck. Acceptance and commitment therapy (ACT) has been shown to be very effective for treating a wide range of disorders, including depression, anxiety, post-traumatic stress disorder, and eating disorders. Instead of trying to escape, avoid, suppress, or change negative emotions, therapists guide you to allow yourself to experience them, without judging them as "bad" or "too painful." This form of therapy can be very effective for people who have tried cognitive therapy (CT) and had little or no success. While CT has you change your thoughts, ACT has you accept them. This was the genesis of ACT, as many people find it easier to accept their thoughts than to try and change them.

You can learn to accept your emotions on your own, or help your child learn how to do it. The goal is to be able to detach from your emotions and watch them peak and decrease, as we discussed in "The Life Cycle of Emotions." In effect, you are observing your own mind, saying, "Oh, look, there's the anxiety. Wow, it's getting bigger and bigger and bigger. Now it's really high. Okay, now it's coming down. And now it's coming down even further." You can do this with any emotion that makes you or your child distressed. Accepting your emotions is equivalent to empathy, and this empathy can be directed toward yourself or toward others.

The "commitment" piece of ACT is about committing to living the life that you want even while experiencing negative emotions. For example, while you may not be able to stop yourself from feeling sadness and anger about your divorce, you can still focus on being the parent that you want to be. You don't have to force these painful emotions to go away in order to focus on your parenting. As many of us are aware, this is a losing battle; the emotions keep coming back, so you continue to postpone your attempts to behave differently. It's like waiting for your depression to pass before you start engaging with friends, eating right, getting more sleep, or exercising. You would be much better off if you accepted feeling depressed and started to do these positive, valued behaviors anyway. Paradoxically, accepting your depression would then likely lead to a decrease in your depression, due to the healthy behaviors you would be doing.

Mira and Emotional Acceptance

Remember Mira and her dance class arrangement from the preceding section? Here is an alternate way that this could have been handled, focusing on emotional acceptance.

Elaine stops what she is doing and looks Mira in the eyes after Mira expresses how upset she is. She says, "I'm so sorry you're upset. I can totally see why you don't like the new arrangement. It was always one way, and you liked it, and now it's another way." Mira's mother isn't saying that she believes that the new arrangement is bad. She isn't saying the new arrangement won't work out or doesn't make sense. She is, however, validating Mira's feelings and saying that they are both important and okay. After a few more minutes of discussion, Mira will likely feel better or may even begin problem solving on her own. If not, her mother can ask, "Do you want to think about ways that we can make this situation better?" Mira will say yes or no. Either way, she will feel heard and understood. Since her emotion wasn't suppressed, it can peak and decrease on its own, and Mira learns that it's okay to feel disappointed, and that disappointment can be survived.

Discipline While Accepting Your Child's Emotions

Let's look at an example of two ways to handle a common parenting scenario:

Your five-year-old is playing with a toy, and his one-year-old brother takes it. Your five-year-old begins to shriek. You say, "Don't be angry; he's a baby. Take this other toy." Your child quiets down. You have inadvertently taught him:

1. Emotions are not okay.

2. Try to avoid feeling them by busying yourself with something else.

3. Don't come to me with your negative emotions, because I don't really want to hear about them.

Now, let's look at this same scenario from a different perspective. Your five-year-old is playing with a toy, and his one-year-old brother takes it. Your five-year-old begins to shriek. You say, "Wow, you seem really angry." Your five-year-old says, "Yeah! He took it!" You say, "I know!" Your five-year-old says something like, "He's a baby, I guess," or goes to take another toy. He may keep talking about how angry he is for a little while or he may not. However, in this second scenario, you have taught your child:

1. Emotions are okay.

2. Emotions are understandable.

3. Emotions don't actually last very long, and they are nothing to be scared of.

4. You can express yourself in this house.

5. You have the ability to problem solve for yourself.

In the first scenario, your child did not get to see that his anger would have peaked and decreased over time without "fixing" it by trying to suppress it and distracting himself from it. As an older child or teen, this child may try to suppress emotions or distract himself from emotions with food, alcohol, or risky behaviors. In the second scenario, your child got to see that he can just accept his emotions, as they are not anything to be scared or ashamed about, and they will go away fairly quickly. This is the child who will also come to you with his issues later in life, because he sees that you accept his emotions without judging them, or him.

PROCESSING EMOTIONS

You may have heard the term *processing emotions*, but what does this really mean? For some people, it's as simple as expressing how they feel in words to someone who listens non-judgmentally. For others, it's talking, or writing, or otherwise expressing their emotions for a long while until they no longer feel as upset. Either way, processing emotions hastens the emotions' increase, peak, and decrease. Your child should not be the one to help you process your emotions; a therapist or a friend can do this. However, you certainly can and should help your child process her emotions in two main ways:

- When you see that your child is experiencing an emotion, ask about what she is feeling.
- When your child shares an emotion, mirror, empathize, and validate. These are all skills we will learn in Chapter 6.

POSITIVE THINKING

We have just learned that it's not helpful to suppress negative feelings. Sadness, anger, and other painful emotions should be accepted, observed, and processed. They should also be empathized with and validated, as we will discuss in Chapter 6. However, do not think that this means you must focus exclusively on discussing negative emotions with your child.

Acceptance of negative emotions is also compatible with trying to look for the positive aspects of situations. In cognitive behavioral therapy, this is called *reframing*. The way that you look at, or frame, situations is the central factor in determining how distressed you feel about them. If your child sees you looking on the bright side, this will become his default way of thinking about the world, which will protect against later negative thinking, anxiety, and depression.

Fortunately for those of us who tend toward negativity, depression, or anxiety, the relatively new field of positive psychology shows that it is possible to train yourself, or your child, to be happy. According to Sonja Lyubomirsky's book *The How of Happiness: A New Approach to Getting the Life You Want*, one of the strongest associations that has been found in happiness research is between gratitude and happiness. Teaching your child to notice and be grateful for small, positive things in his life is one of the most effective ways to ensure that your child can transcend the way he is innately wired and become the happiest he can be.

There are also many other ways to teach yourself to be happier. Happiness is a choice and comes from specific concrete activities and ways of thinking. Here are eleven questions that you can ask your child in order to increase her happiness on a regular basis. Eventually your child will internalize these questions and ask them inside her own head, both now and as an adult.

"What was your favorite part of today?"

This is a good question to ask at bedtime, to help your child feel content and happy before sleep. It also instills a habit of focusing on the best thing that happened in any given day rather than the worst.

"What are you grateful for?"

This is a good question for the dinner table, where every family member can say what she is grateful for that day. There is a strong correlation between happiness and gratitude, so instill a gratitude habit as early as you can.

"What are you going to do about that?"

When a child comes to you with a problem, ask this question in a warm and curious tone. Give your child a chance to work problems out on her own, and give her the gift of your confidence. If your child says "I don't know," you can say, "I'm not sure either. Let's try to figure it out together." Happy people think of problems as surmountable, and think of themselves as effective problem solvers.

"How did that make you feel?"

Many people don't know how to notice and express their own emotions, which means they cannot process their feelings or obtain support from others by expressing how they feel. "How did that make you feel?" is a great question to ask when your child comes to you with a concern, instead of either dismissing and invalidating (e.g., "That's not that bad") or fixing (e.g., "Let Mommy get you some ice!").

Expressing curiosity about your children's emotions makes them curious about their own emotions, and also shows respect, since you're not just assuming that you know what they feel. This question shows that you think of your child as a separate entity with her own emotions, desires, goals, and plans. The more you demonstrate confidence in your child's ability to navigate the world successfully, the more confident and effective your child will feel.

"What do you think he/she feels?"

Empathy is a skill best taught at home early in life. A child who understands how to be empathic toward others will be a happier person; he will have stronger interpersonal relationships, feel proud of himself for thinking of others, and derive more meaning from life.

"How can we look on the bright side?"

In any situation, you can teach your child that there are positives. You can also teach kids the expression "making lemonade out of a lemon" and ask them how you can make lemonade out of a bad situation, like, "You fell and hurt yourself, so that's a lemon, but you got a Tinkerbell Band-Aid, and that's lemonade!"

"What part of that can we learn more about?"

In any TV show, book, trip outside the house, or interpersonal interaction there is something to learn more about. Most parents feel that they use their smartphones or computers too much around their kids, but here is a way that you can use your electronic devices to show your child that life is full of learning opportunities. Happy people are curious and are always learning. So when you watch TV and someone says "Bonjour," you can look up pictures of France or find a French song on YouTube. When your child realizes that this question means that you're about to research something new and special with him, he will look excited whenever you ask it.

"What do you want to do on the weekend/on vacation/tonight?"

Research shows that anticipation of positive experiences brings more happiness than the experiences themselves. Once your child is old enough to realize that tomorrow is not today, start instilling a habit of positive anticipation of small pleasures. A child who is excited all week to get frozen yogurt on the weekend is a happy child, just as an adult who plans a vacation six months in advance is happier during those six months.

"What can we do to help/to make someone happy?"

Bringing your child along to visit a sick relative, or to volunteer at a soup kitchen is a wonderful gift. Your child will feel even prouder of his behavior if he is the one to think up the nice thing that can be done (e.g., baking cookies to deliver, drawing a card). Research shows that giving releases oxytocin and endorphins, so it's like a natural "high" to which your child can become "addicted." Involve your child in charitable activities, as charitable giving is a form of altruism that is also linked directly to happiness. Incorporate a spirit of generosity into your child's daily life. Whenever you're out, buy something little for someone else. When you color, make a picture for someone else. Giving things to others makes people happier than buying things for themselves and enriches interpersonal relationships.

"What do you want to do outside today?"

Getting outside with your child each day is a wonderful way to promote physical activity. Exercise releases endorphins and, as some research indicates, is as effective at treating depression as medication. And the most powerful way that you can teach your child about exercise is to do it yourself. Research indicates that children whose parents exercise are more likely to exercise themselves. And sunlight can also help boost mood and regulate circadian rhythms, which leads to better sleep.

"When do you feel happiest?"

If you direct your children's attention to the experiences that they most enjoy, they will start to realize that they can choose to increase their time spent in activities that make them feel best about themselves. According to researcher Mihaly Csikszentmihalyi, "flow" is the state where people find an activity so enjoyable and rewarding that they become completely immersed in it, losing all sense of time and feeling completely in the moment. If your child is lucky enough to have found an activity that puts him in "flow," it is helpful for you to point this out and allow your child enough time to attain this state. (And yes, even video games teach collaboration, problem solving, and logical reasoning!) The best-case scenario is for your child to find a career that puts him in "flow," since then, as the saying goes, he will never "work" a day in his life.

Take your job as your child's happiness role model seriously. Even if you are feeling very negative about your life and your future post-divorce, you still need to show your child that a positive worldview is possible. You and your co-parent are the most influential figures in your child's life. Showing your child that happiness is a choice and that there are proactive, specific ways to be happy can be one of the best things you do as a parent.

Key points from this chapter:

- Emotions are not "good" or "bad"; they just are

- If emotions are suppressed, they never truly recede

- If expressed and accepted, emotions have a natural peak, and then they decrease

- Accepting your own emotions is just as important as accepting your child's emotions

- You can train yourself and your child to look for the positive in life, which will help both of you become happier and more resilient

CHAPTER 6

COMMUNICATION SKILLS

You probably can think of times when you felt very distressed and talking to someone else calmed you down and left you feeling confident and better able to handle your issues. In these cases, it is likely that your conversation partner used the skills of mirroring, curiosity, empathy, and validation. Some people know these skills innately from witnessing them at home, and other people learn them later in life.

The way that you communicate with your child can make or break your relationship. From the smallest non-verbal child to an adult, people want to feel heard, understood, and accepted by their parents. This is particularly important when a child feels insecure or threatened, as he will during or after a divorce. Your child is undergoing what is probably the biggest stressor in his life to date, and may not feel that he is your priority anymore. Your communication methods set the stage for your child to view your divorce as a sad event rather than the cataclysm that destroyed life as she knew it.

The parent-child relationship provides the basic foundation for a child to learn how to interact with others, such as peers, and later, in adult intimate relationships. Thankfully, there are simple skills you can learn that will help you communicate in a healthier way with your child. These specific, teachable communication methods can help your child to learn about, process, and accept his feelings, while also feeling strong enough to change how he responds to his feelings. You can use these skills with children of all ages, during even the most heated encounters. All of these techniques help show your child that you love him, and will defuse tension and anger so that you can truly hear what your child wants to tell you. The basic communication techniques that we will cover are mirroring, curiosity, empathy, and validation. It is also essential to take responsibility for your own words and actions, and to apologize when appropriate. Lastly, it is important to understand how and when to use praise.

Keep in mind that you may be changing how you interact with your child if you incorporate these techniques into your conversations. Children often feel off-balance when parents try something new, because they don't know the new "rules." If you try some of these new techniques without discussing them beforehand with your child, she may look at you strangely and may even act rude or mocking. Don't let this dissuade you from communicating in a new and healthier way.

To get your children on board and to help prevent them from feeling that you're manipulating them or acting "fake," it would be wonderful to have a brief discussion with your kids where you say that you're going to try to start talking in a different way so that you can be nicer and more positive. Your children will likely be surprised and pleased that you think enough of them and your relationship with them to try and change your own behavior. The younger the child is, the more quickly and enthusiastically he will respond to your new communication style. Toddlers and preschoolers may not even remember a time before you communicated this way, and it will rapidly become your household norm. Preteens and teenagers may make fun of you using these skills, but they will appreciate them and will slowly begin to use them as well.

MIRRORING: NON-JUDGMENTAL ACCEPTANCE OF YOUR CHILD'S FEELINGS.

"When people talk, listen completely.
Most people never listen."
—Ernest Hemingway

The first and most basic communication skill that will help you better communicate with your child is mirroring. Mirroring is when you repeat back what your child has said. In the case of a pre-verbal child, you say what you think they mean. Here is an example of mirroring. Your eight-year-old says to you, "You never let me do anything! Daddy lets me watch TV two hours every night!" You would simply respond, "You feel like I don't let you do anything, and Daddy lets you watch TV every night." This makes your child feel understood, and, even more importantly, it stops you from responding in one of these typical, unhelpful ways:

- Defensiveness: "Well, Daddy doesn't have to do homework with you!"
- Counterattack: "Maybe with Daddy you act nicer!"
- Dismissing: "Yeah right. He tells me he limits you to an hour."

The purpose of mirroring is to show your child that you understand his point. This is the basic foundation for a calm discussion. If you show your child that you at least hear what he is saying, your child will not escalate the situation as rapidly, if at all. Many children calm down immediately and expand on what they mean. Mirroring is easy once you get the hang of it. Best of all, you can usually see your child's relief when, instead of correcting her or defending yourself, you just repeat non-judgmentally what she has said.

EMPATHY

"I do not ask the wounded person how he feels . . .
I myself become the wounded person."
—Walt Whitman, *Song of Myself*

Empathy is the basis of all intimate interpersonal relationships. When you empathize with someone, you truly understand her perspective, no matter whether or not you agree with her thoughts or opinions. Empathy, if expressed well, instantly defuses even the most explosive, high-conflict situation. It's like a magic potion that makes others calm down, listen to you, and feel connected with you.

Empathy can be relationship-changing, but it can also be very difficult, especially when you're under stress or you're trying to empathize with someone you really don't understand at all. In this chapter we will explore how to empathize with your kids in a variety of situations, particularly those times when you're feeling frustrated, anxious, and angry, and especially when your child is doing things that you find incomprehensible. Once you master the skill of empathizing, you can use it in any situation that arises where you want to connect to your child or defuse a conflict.

Empathizing is the first step in addressing your children's intense emotional reactions, or their difficult, destructive, or otherwise frustrating behavior. This flies in the face of how the majority of parents respond when a child acts upset. Generally, when parents see their kids acting extremely upset, or behaving "badly," the parents feel distressed, angry and powerless. They try to jump right in and remedy things, often by telling kids they shouldn't feel or act that way, problem solving, telling their kids about alternate ways that they can behave, and even giving them consequences or punishments with the goal of helping them "shape up."

Although less sensitive or easier-going children will comply with demands, even with a smile, these efforts often go poorly. This is because there is no foundation of empathy, and your child does not feel that you understand his experience. And if your child doesn't feel understood, he is less likely to listen to your solutions, try any of your alternative behaviors, or learn anything from the consequences. Instead, he will detach from you, assuming that you have no idea what he feels or thinks. He may also feel alone, sad, angry, and unloved.

Be Curious

If you genuinely have no idea how your child is feeling, ask her directly, with warm curiosity. Curiosity is a wonderful and flattering way to make a child, or anyone, feel that her thoughts and feelings are interesting to you. Express your curiosity openly, like:

- "I'm interested in what you're feeling, but I don't think I understand."
- "Can you explain to me how you feel?"
- "I'm curious about what you are/were feeling."
- "I've never been in this situation. How do you feel?"

In all of these examples, the key is that you are not judging your child for not communicating effectively, or, worse, for having feelings that don't make sense. As we already learned in Chapter 5, emotions don't make sense; they just exist.

VALIDATION

To fully understand validation, we have to first use empathy. As you just read, empathy means acknowledging and understanding another person's thoughts and feelings. Validating takes this understanding one step further, as you are now saying that it makes sense to you that the person feels that way. Once you're primed to try to validate your child, you may even be able to think of additional reasons why your child's emotion is logical given the situation. Remember, in order to validate your child, you do *not* have to say that you'd react the same way. You do have to say that it makes sense to you that your child, in your child's unique situation, feels the way that he does.

MIRRORING, EMPATHY, AND VALIDATION IN ACTION

The wonderful thing about mirroring, empathy, and validation is they are stand-alone techniques to help your child, meaning that they are often useful in and of themselves without then having to fix the situation in any other way. Often it is enough for your child to feel heard and understood, and she then feels strong enough to solve her problem on her own, or to accept that it has no easy solution. Sometimes your child will ask your advice or welcome your input on a difficult issue, but only after you empathize and validate.

Here are some examples of mirroring, empathizing, and validation with children across a range of ages:

Preschooler: "Waah, you hurt me with the comb! You're mean!"
You: "Aw, you got hurt with the comb."

In this relatively simple situation, all your child may need is you mirroring his feelings. If you do this, your child will likely calm down fairly quickly.

Here's a more emotional and complicated situation with an elementary-school-age child:

Child: "You're making me go to Daddy's even though I don't want to! I hate you."
You: "I see. You really don't want to go to Daddy's, and you're mad at me. That makes sense."

DON'T COMPARE!

Often, parents who experienced divorce as children themselves are committed to making their divorce an easier experience for their own kids. They try to keep the divorce as conflict-free as possible, and to keep their child's routines intact. Then, they often feel bewildered and hurt when their children are just as angry, sad, and accusatory as they were toward their own parents, and even significantly more so!

If you are a child of divorce, don't fall into the trap of assuming that you and your child are undergoing identical experiences. Comparing your experiences, feelings, and reactions to your child's can often backfire, especially if you feel that you coped more effectively, or if you believe your own situation was more difficult. In previous generations, children did not feel as able to express themselves as openly to their parents, so it is actually a positive thing if your child feels comfortable to express his anger and resentment more openly than you might have done as a child.

Another common occurrence is parental downward comparison. When a parent experienced abuse, parental alcoholism or mental illness, the death of a parent at a young age, a major childhood illness or injury, or any other trauma, sometimes he compares his own experience and coping style to his child's current coping style, and the child comes out lacking. It is easy to think of your divorce as a minimal stressor on your child if you yourself were sexually abused by an alcoholic parent, or had a parent die when you were very young. If you were caring for your younger siblings as a teenager because your mother suffered from debilitating depression, it is likely to anger you when your own teenage child complains about waiting another year to get his own car.

Whether or not your situation as a child was "better" or "worse" than your child's situation is irrelevant. Divorce, like all interpersonal situations, is very subjective. Remember, your child does not see your own childhood juxtaposed next to his on a split screen. He is only cognizant of his own experience, and he compares his current situation only to previous situations that he has known, and to situations experienced by his peer group. If he is the only person he knows whose parents have divorced, it is no consolation to him that his parent's parents divorced.

Further, there is no chance that your child will learn new coping skills because he has heard that you, at his age, were able to cope well. You have likely already witnessed the emotional shutdown and retreat that occur when you tell your child how good he has it compared to you, although many parents keep reiterating this information in the unrealistic hope that, one day, their child will try to change his behavior to be more like theirs. If your child could cope better with the divorce, he already would be. Hearing how responsible, well-behaved, and appreciative you were as a child will either seem like a lie to your child, or make him feel like a failure in your eyes and in his own. Lastly, if your child feels that he will always be compared to you and will come up short, he will withdraw and prefer not to engage at all. This way, he can avoid being compared unfavorably to you and facing your disappointment.

My Daughter Doesn't Know How Good She Has It

Liz, 38, writes: "My parents got divorced, too, and boy, was that awful. They would scream and yell about money, and about my dad not coming to see us. The situation was just terrible. My kids experience nothing like that. Everything is calm and orderly. My ex and I split custody right down the middle. Even still, my eleven-year-old daughter Maddie tells me I ruined her life and she can't understand why I couldn't keep my marriage together. Can you believe she talks to me that way? I don't understand her at all."

———————————

Dear Liz, that does sound like a frustrating situation. However, it seems like you're falling into a common trap of comparing your own situation to your daughter's, and judging her for behaving worse than you did at the same age. This is not helpful in the current situation, and, if you have shared these feelings with your daughter, your daughter likely feels judged and criticized.

I will do a little role-play exercise where I imagine what a conversation between the two of you may look like if you were to use empathy and validation to talk to and connect with your daughter in a more meaningful way.

Liz: "Hey, Maddie, I want to talk to you about before, when you were telling me I couldn't keep my marriage together and I ruined your life. That hurt my feelings, so I wasn't able to talk to you in the moment, but now I want to try and understand how you feel."

Maddie: "Look, whatever I'm sorry, but I meant it. I feel like Dad never did anything to you and now I don't have a normal life. I can't even do dance anymore because you can't drive me there. I'm the only freak I know."

Liz: "You feel like you're the only one with such a difficult life, and that it's my fault that the marriage didn't work out. You're upset and angry. I'm sorry."

Maddie: "Yeah, I'm upset and angry. And it's at you."

Liz: "You're really mad at me. I understand. I can see why you would be mad if you think the divorce was all my fault, and I can see why you're mad that I can't drive you to dance because I'm working more now. I would feel the same way if I were in your position. I actually felt that my parents' divorce was because of my dad, and it took me a long time to realize it was just a terrible thing that happened, and it wasn't all his fault. I am also really sorry about dance."

Maddie (calmer): "Well, I don't know. Whatever. It's not a big deal, Mom."

You know that it's still a big deal to Maddie, but your daughter is trying to say that she feels a little closer to you after talking. In this scenario, you've successfully avoided the traps of comparing your own "better" behavior to your daughter's rude behavior, and you also didn't engage with your daughter's mocking tone. By concentrating on empathy and validation, you were able to make your daughter feel a little bit more understood, which is why the tension drained out of the encounter by the end of the exchange.

Note that I am not saying you should minimize Maddie's distress about not getting driven to dance class anymore. Following this conversation, it would be a great idea to initiate a conversation with Maddie about possible ways for her to still be able to go to dance class, like finding a studio closer to home, or getting a friend's mom to drive her, or finding a weekend class. This would certainly help Maddie feel even more understood and prioritized. But finding a way to get Maddie to dance was not, nor should it have been, the focus of this conversation. If you got sucked into an argument about how you could, in fact, drive her to dance if she rearranged her life in a different way, or defended why you can't, or chastised Maddie for her ingratitude for everything that you do for her, both of you would leave the interaction feeling angry and unheard. The first step in any difficult interaction is empathy and validation, which pave the way for a calmer discussion later on. No matter how important dance is to Maddie, feeling understood and loved by her mother is even more important. I hope you can use this example to guide how you communicate better with Maddie in the future.

EMPATHIZE WITH AND VALIDATE YOUR CHILD'S DESIRE TO TALK ABOUT YOUR CO-PARENT

Most kids in divorced families are unsure about how much you want to hear them talk about their other parent. Even if you are extraordinarily angry with your co-parent, you need to show your child that she is able to discuss her other parent with you openly, without you responding negatively. Remember, if your child is led to reject one parent, she is rejecting half of herself, and her self-esteem will suffer accordingly. As a child ages, she can make her own judgments about what qualities she likes and wants to emulate from both you and her other parent, but at this age, it is healthiest for your child to view both parents as positive overall.

If you're honest with yourself, it can be a tossup whether it is harder to hear your child talk positively or negatively about your co-parent. On some level, particularly if your divorce has been acrimonious, it is natural to want to be your child's favored parent. But hearing that your child dislikes or feels hurt by your co-parent can be even more upsetting. It is best to take a neutral attitude toward your co-parent when speaking to your child. Do not act as though your co-parent is wrong even if you yourself have qualms about his or her behavior (see Chapter 7).

HOW DO YOU EMPATHIZE WHEN YOUR CHILD IS RUDE?

There are some situations when it is particularly difficult to marshal the inner resources necessary to empathize with your child. When a child is rude or attacking, it can severely test a parent's patience and ability to stay calm and empathic. Remember that empathy does not in any way mean that you should allow your child to speak rudely to you. However, I encourage you to respond to the content of your child's statement first, no matter how rudely it is expressed, and then respond to the rudeness later on in the conversation. In other words, once you have truly heard, empathized with, and validated your child, it is important to address the disrespectful manner in which he conveyed his feelings to you.

Some parents face the opposite problem of feeling too guilty or sad for their child to focus on addressing their child's rude behavior. If this is your issue, please keep in mind that it does your child a disservice to learn that nothing he says hurts anyone's feelings. This will hamper him when relating to others, whether it's peers now or intimate partners later in life. Here's an example of John, age seven, talking to his mother, Pamela. Pamela is trying to be empathic and validating but is also helping John realize that his words can hurt other people, which is a valuable and essential lesson.

John: "I hate you! I hate you and your stupid boyfriend."

Pamela: "I hear you. You are really mad at me and Harry."

John: "Your stupid boyfriend is fat like you, no wonder you like him."

Pamela: "I think you are really angry about me having someone else in my life. That makes sense. After all, he does take up some of my time now."

John: "Like all your time."

Pamela: "I get it, you're upset that I'm spending too much time with Harry. You wish I was spending more time with you instead. I will try to have our special Mom and John time every week again, like we had been doing before Harry. Would that be better?"

John: "Yeah, I guess."

Pamela: "But listen, it is not okay that you just called me and Harry fat, or that you called him stupid. That hurt my feelings, and it would hurt his feelings if he heard you say that, too. If you want to say something that is not very nice about how someone looks or how smart they are, you need to keep it in your own head. You can think I am stupid or fat if you want, but it's not nice to say it out loud to me, and it does not make me feel good."

John: "You're not fat or stupid, Mom."

Pamela: "Thanks, John."

TAKE RESPONSIBILITY AND APOLOGIZE

One of the most important things you can do for your child is to be aware of your own behavior and its impact on others, and take responsibility and apologize for any negative outcomes. Adult children of divorced parents frequently feel that their parents tried to minimize their own bad behaviors throughout the divorce, and blamed their co-parents for any negative consequences on the children. This leads to a lack of closeness and trust between children and parents that can continue into adulthood. It seems to kids like it is more important to their parents to save face and put a positive spin on their own actions than to understand how their kids are feeling and engage honestly with them.

I recommend that parents get in the habit of apologizing at least once per week to their children, whether it's for minor daily occurrences like snapping at them when you lose your patience or for larger issues like throwing their lives into disarray with the divorce. Apologizing for the divorce does not mean that you don't think it's the right decision but that you recognize how difficult it's been for your child and are not trying to minimize her pain. These apologies, whether for big or small things, should be stated directly and sincerely. The point is not to guilt-trip your child into assuring you that she is fine. The point is to acknowledge and "own," meaning honestly take responsibility for, your actions and their impact on your loved ones, particularly your child.

Parents commonly want their children to be honest and accept responsibility for their actions, whether it's hitting a sibling or being rude to a parent. Yet very few parents do this themselves. You are not above taking ownership of your actions and their consequences just by virtue of your age or status as an adult. In fact, it is even more important for adults to own their behaviors so that children can see firsthand how to do it.

In order for children to have functional and happy intimate relationships as adults, it is of primary importance that they learn how to interact in positive, functional ways at home. Then, as adults, they will be able to deploy these skills automatically and unconsciously when they interact with others. If kids haven't seen others act this way, they don't know what words to use when taking ownership or apologizing, or how to act while saying them. In case this is your situation, and it is difficult for you to apologize for own your actions because you never saw this when growing up, read the sidebar "How to Apologize in Four Steps."

How to Apologize in Four Steps

We will use the example of you apologizing to your child, but these steps can be used in all of your interpersonal relationships. Apologizing is a skill just like any other, and, with practice, you can become more comfortable and adept at apologizing, and being less defensive.

1. Use specifics. Just saying "sorry" doesn't sound thoughtful or sincere. "I'm sorry I yelled at you during dinner" is much better. Better still, note the consequence of your behavior in your child, like, "I noticed that you seemed sad after I yelled."

2. Ask how your child feels. A tone of warm curiosity shows your child that you are genuinely interested in her thoughts and feelings, not just pushing your own agenda or saving face. You can say, "What did you feel when I yelled?" This gives your child a chance to both express herself and clear up any incorrect assumptions you may have had. For instance, your child might answer, "I wasn't sad that you yelled, but I felt guilty for bothering you." This would help you learn more

about your behavior's effect on your child. If your child says, "I don't know," or "I don't want to talk about it," don't lose heart. She is still listening to what you say and still appreciates your attempts at repair.

3. Use empathy and validation. Here's an example: "I can understand why you would have felt guilty for bothering me, since I told you to be quiet and stop stressing me out." Remember, this is not the time to bring up anything negative about your child or teach her how to change her behavior. Don't risk your child closing off by saying, "You know, though, you were being pretty loud. You need to remember to use your inside voice at the table."

4. Show that you're committed to change. Come up with a plan to address this situation in the future, which shows that this episode has taught you something. Here, you could say, "Even if you're being loud at the table in the future, and even if I'm feeling stressed, I'm going to try to ask you nicely to lower your voice rather than yell at you."

The Benefits of Apologizing

Apologizing to your child and owning your actions have many positive effects:

- It establishes a more level playing field, in which you and your child are not "adult" and "child" but two human beings who sometimes mess up. This can lead to a closer and more connected relationship.

- Your child learns from you exactly how to take responsibility for his actions and apologize.

- Your child feels that you have taken him and his emotions seriously, to the point that you regret your behavior.

All of these are great reasons to get into the habit of openly assessing your own behaviors on a regular basis and owning and apologizing for behaviors that have hurt others. Don't dilute your apologies with "I didn't mean to make you upset," as this can be perceived as trying to wiggle out of accepting responsibility. Instead, simply apologize for the effects of your actions.

WHEN PRAISE CAN HURT

You may be tempted to praise your child more frequently in the aftermath of a divorce, for all the best-intended reasons: You want to buoy your child's self-esteem, show how much you love him, and recognize and reinforce "positive" ways of dealing with divorce stress. It is also so unexpected and relieving when a child appears to be unfazed by the divorce that you may find yourself praising his ability to be cheerful or adaptable.

Some parents also snap at their children much more during a divorce, because they feel so stressed and anxious. They feel guilty, and indulge in excessive praise in an attempt to compensate for treating their child poorly. No matter why you rely on praise, it is important to realize that overuse of praise may have the unintentional results of pushing your child away from you and also actually decreasing his self-esteem.

Let's say that your child is acting especially flexible about a change in schedule. You may feel very relieved, and say, "You're such an easy kid. You're really a good girl, going with the flow like that." You may be feeling very warm and loving to your child, and your child may seem happy, too. But there is a lot of potential for this interaction to make your child feel anxious and insecure. Here are a few of the things that your child could be thinking:

- "Mommy would really be disappointed if she knew that I was secretly upset about not going today. She loves me because I'm a good kid, but I'm not *really* a good kid."

- "Yeah, I was fine this time because I didn't even want to go to Dad's. But what if next time I do get upset and Mom doesn't love me anymore?"

- "The way to make people happy is to go with the flow, so I better go with the flow no matter what."

In *Between Parent and Child*, psychologist Haim G. Ginott discusses why children often misbehave immediately after being praised for being "good." He notes that kids often feel guilty that a parent considers them "good" when they know the truth—that they were just thinking something "bad" or are not always "good." By misbehaving, they hope to show their parents the truth and not feel that their parents only love them based on an impression that is incorrect. I think that this phenomenon could also be explained by a child testing a parent to see if the parent will still love him even if he acts "bad."

Key points from this chapter:

- Mirroring is repeating what your child has just stated, even if you don't agree with it

- Curiosity is used to explore more about how your child feels.

- Empathy is when you truly understand your child's perspective

- Validation is when you convey that your child's feelings make sense to you

- Mirroring, empathy, and validation can defuse many tense and difficult conversations

- Empathy and validation can be used even in tough parenting situations like rudeness or tantrums

- Owning your actions and apologizing for them allow your child to feel closer to you and to learn these skills for himself

CHAPTER 7

HOW TO TALK ABOUT YOUR CO-PARENT

People do not divorce without knowing that their marriage is irrevocably broken, and it takes a lot to get to that point. Years of conflict, loneliness, bitterness, and anger are the backdrop for divorce, and there is no way to pretend that these feelings just don't exist. For many, even thinking of their co-parent is horribly painful and causes almost unbearable rage and sadness. Yet, I am going to entreat you to try your hardest to compartmentalize these feelings and commit to talking about your co-parent in a way that can help your children psychologically acclimate to the divorce in the healthiest way possible.

CHANGE OF TERMINOLOGY

In *Mom's House, Dad's House: Making Two Homes for Your Child,* Dr. Isolina Ricci discusses how it can be a psychological game-changer to use different language in regard to your divorce. There are two very important changes of terminology that can really reframe how you and your children think about divorce. The first is calling your ex-spouse your "co-parent" or "children's mother/father," and the second is saying that your child "lives with" both parents, rather than lives with one and visits the other, no matter what the duration of the stay at each home is. Let's examine why each of these is so important and helpful.

Co-Parent, Not Ex

As you've probably noticed, throughout this book, I have been referring to your ex-spouse as your co-parent. This is a variation on Ricci's suggestion to call your ex-spouse "my child's father/mother." Feel free to use whichever term works for you or whichever arises naturally in conversation with your child and with others. Either way, changing how you refer to your ex-spouse is essential for reframing how you think of him or her. I like saying co-parent because every time you say it, you're reminded that you're on a team with this person. Rather than saying "ex," which calls to mind a failed marriage, you are emphasizing your effort to parent your child as a team.

This change of terminology is designed to be all-encompassing, with you making your best effort to think about your ex-spouse as your co-parent, and to use that phrase when talking to your friends and family members, as well as your child. This language change may seem silly, but changing the way you talk about something can change how you think about it. Over time, this verbal change will help change your view of your child's other parent into just that—her other parent—rather than a person who used to be married to you.

Living With, Not Visiting

Another important change suggested by Dr. Ricci is the idea of each child having two homes. Rather than conceptualizing a child as "living with" one parent and "visiting" the other, it is healthier for your child and your co-parenting relationship to state that the child lives with one parent X amount of the time and the other parent Y amount of the time. This also helps the co-parent who gets less time with the child to still feel involved and essential. If you feel like your child is only a visitor, this makes you feel that your relationship is peripheral, not the central parent-child relationship in the child's life. This leads to sadness, increased distance between the parent and the child, and also conflict between the parents, one of whom thinks he or she is the "real" or "main" parent, and the other, who feels marginalized.

When a child is "living with" you, even only for a couple of days per week, this triggers feelings of family and permanence. You're more likely to give your child his own personal space, you have more toys and personal effects at your home, and thus your child is also likely to feel less like a transitory presence. Saying "I live with my dad Friday, Saturday, and Sunday this week" sounds closer and more homey than saying, "I'm visiting my dad this weekend." When international students go abroad for the semester, they have a "host family" whom they "live with." Your child is closer to you than an exchange student! No matter how many days and nights he spends with Mom or Dad, your child deserves to feel like he has a home with each parent.

BADMOUTHING YOUR CO-PARENT

It is essential that you do not blame your co-parent for the divorce, as we discussed in the previous chapter. This includes passive-aggressive remarks like, "I guess some people think differently about commitment" or "Well, at least nothing much will change in *his* life!" As you've heard, children are sponges, and they soak in not only what you explicitly say about their other parent but also the tone in which you say it. It is very painful for children to hear one parent badmouth another. The kids are caught in the middle, which is a stressful and unfair place for them to be. A child deserves to be able to feel loyalty to both parents. This is tough if it seems like the only way to support one parent is to reject the other.

One seven-year-old son of a DrPsychMom.com reader said that hearing one parent talk badly about the other is "like having someone say your favorite song is stupid." This is a very insightful way to showcase how hurtful it is for a child to hear a loved parent be criticized or mocked by the other parent. The child is caught in a no-win situation—if he agrees with the badmouthing parent, then he feels ashamed for betraying his other parent, but if he defends the parent who is being badmouthed, he risks offending the badmouther. Since children already feel insecure and anxious about keeping their parents' love after a divorce, it can feel impossible to speak up for one parent if this means possibly losing a relationship with the other.

Children are very literal, and therefore they do not know if one parent is exaggerating the deficiencies of the other parent, or if the badmouthing parent is using hyperbole. For example, if one parent says that the other "doesn't know how to care take of you," a child may worry that she is in danger with that parent. Also, an expression like, "Your dad is making me crazy!" is not taken as an expression of anger and frustration but a literal remark that can make a child very anxious.

Maura and George

Here is an example of how one parent blaming another can have an extremely destructive effect on children. Maura, 45, and George, 53, have been separated for six months and plan to divorce in another six, as per the laws of their state. They have two daughters, Amy, 17, and Elana, 16. The girls are allied with their mother, who believes and states openly that George was never a "real" husband to her. By this she means that he was uncommunicative and unsupportive during even her most painful moments during their 21 years together, such as when she was diagnosed with lupus, or when her mother passed away. Maura often revisits these perceived betrayals, and discusses them with her therapist, her friends, and, to a lesser extent, her daughters. Both girls feel that their mother is the victim in the divorce, and both barely speak to their father. Amy in particular is angry with her father, and has even refused his assistance with her college tuition.

Maura is worried about what both girls will end up thinking about romantic relationships, since Amy doesn't date and says she "never wants to get married," and Elana gets involved in very brief, volatile relationships characterized by a lot of "drama" and fighting, where she gets disappointed with and disgusted by her boyfriends' treatment of her. Maura interprets her girls' dysfunctional attitudes toward long-term relationships as a sad but inevitable result of their observations of their ineffectual father. Despite her intelligence and love for her daughters, she is unable to realize that her own badmouthing of George is a primary contributor to the girls' distance from him and distrust of men in general.

If Maura were to openly discuss with her therapist that she allows the girls to overhear her talking badly about George to her friends, and that she in fact sometimes uses the girls as sounding boards to vent her frustration about her "wasted" twenty-one years of marriage, it is likely that her therapist would bring her attention to how this behavior is unintentionally hurting her daughters. If Maura were to keep her disappointment to herself and allow her girls to make their own judgments about their father, it is likely that they would be able to form a relationship with him that could enrich their lives.

Parental Alienation: The Worst-Case Scenario

Parental alienation, a term created by Richard A. Gardner, MD in the 1980s and discussed extensively in his book *The Parental Alienation Syndrome*, occurs when one parent destroys the relationship between the child and the other parent. This can be done via blatant lies about the other parent ("Daddy never wanted you") or more subtle cues such as sighing and seeming upset when a parent calls on the phone, or even just ignoring and refusing to talk about the other parent, which signals to a child that loving or thinking about this parent is not acceptable. Although Gardner equates parental alienation to brainwashing, he also makes the important distinction that a child actively participates in the rejection of the "hated" parent, rather than being passively programmed. The child even extends the denigration and bashing of the "hated" parent, using extremely hostile and hateful words, and insisting that her hatred of one parent is her own idea. However, there is usually very little basis for the child's hatred, and the child uses the other parent's words when describing how terrible the offending parent is.

Parental alienation occurs in the context of a pre-divorce parent-child relationship that was mutually loving, not one where there was abuse or neglect and therefore a real reason that a child might fear or dislike his parent. (In actuality, the majority of children still love abusive or neglectful parents and wish to spend time with them.) Despite this history of closeness, the child begins to reject his parent entirely after the divorce, and often explains this rejection in terms of what he hears from his other parent, such as complaining that Dad is "crazy," or that Mom is "self-centered." This hatred goes beyond common feelings of anger that children commonly express toward their parents at times. The words that children use to describe this parent are those that they have heard the other parent (or the other parent's family) use.

Parental alienation has many psychological explanations. Children want to keep the love of their primary caretaker (who is most often the one doing the alienating of the other parent), and they have intuited that the only way to do this is to join the primary caretaking parent in his or her hatred of the other parent. Whenever the child speaks poorly of the alienated parent, his primary caretaker feels validated and seems happier. However, when a child tries to share positive thoughts or feelings about the alienated parent, he quickly realizes that this causes his primary caretaker to experience anger and unhappiness, directed both at the child and his other parent.

Additionally, children are extremely suggestible, as I discuss in Chapter 13, in the section "When Your Child Accuses You or Your Co-Parent of Mistreatment." If one parent consistently denigrates the other and brings up stories in which the offending parent is portrayed as a villain, a child will begin to believe this narrative, irrespective of his own observations and personal experience with the parent. In addition to directly badmouthing the other parent, an alienating parent can advance his or her agenda by utilizing more indirect tactics, such as isolation, ruining time with the other parent, and expressing fear of the hated parent.

Alienated children often feel and demonstrate a complete lack of love or affection toward the alienated parent, and echo the complaints that they have heard from their other parent. Here are the symptoms of parental alienation, outlined by Dr. Gardner in *The Parental Alienation Syndrome*:

1. The child denigrates the alienated parent, using verbal epithets and defiant behavior

2. The child offers weak or irrational reasons for her hatred, often in terms that she doesn't understand or don't seem to be childlike (e.g., "I hate Mom because she doesn't feed us healthy food")

3. The child shows no ambivalence, as people do in most relationships, but only hatred

4. The child insists that he independently decided to reject the alienated parent

5. The child protects the alienating parent, who is viewed as only good

6. The child shows no guilt about his mean behavior to the alienated parent

7. The child describes situations that occurred when he was very young or that occurred between the two parents only (meaning he overheard others talk about these situations)

8. The child treats the friends and/or extended family of the alienated parent with hostility

Parental alienation is the most tragic and destructive possible consequence of a parent talking badly about the other. Often, the relationship with an alienated parent is never repaired, or is repaired much later in life, when there is no chance to recapture a lost childhood together. If your child acts hostile and hateful toward you on a regular basis, and says things about you that he could only possibly have overheard from your co-parent or friends or family members of your co-parent, it is important to nip this potential parental alienation in the bud.

One path is to try to work with your co-parent in mediation or, better, family therapy, to negotiate more time with your child and an agreement for both co-parents to stop talking about one another to the children. Next, Richard A. Warshak, author of *Divorce Poison: How to Protect Your Family from Bad-mouthing and Brainwashing*, encourages alienated parents to be proactive in getting their points across to their children, namely, that they love them and want to have a relationship with them. Many alienated parents feel trapped and hopeless, and do not know how to win back their child's love. Working with psychologists and attorneys who specialize in parental alienation can also help you before your relationship with your child is irrevocably harmed.

An alienating parent is not an evil person. In many cases, this person truly believes that his or her co-parent is a horrible, cruel, or otherwise damaged person and that the children will derive no benefit from being close to this parent. The marriage may have been filled with heartbreaking betrayals and egregious behavior by both parties, and the rage and resentment that the alienating parent feels are obscuring the ability to separate the co-parent as a spouse from the co-parent as a parent.

Research now shows that parental alienation can be helped along by the "hated" parent, who grows more depressed, angry, and passive in response to the child's rejection, opening himself or herself up to further rejection from the child. Alienation can happen even in the absence of badmouthing, and can happen bi-directionally between parents. There are many complex factors in the child's environment that lead to a child deciding to reject one parent and blame him or her for the divorce and later issues. Thus, even if there is no conscious or unconscious badmouthing, a child may still reject one parent. In this case, both parents should agree to bring the child to family therapy in order to ensure that the child is able to maintain two loving parent-child relationships in the wake of the divorce.

"GOOD-ENOUGH" PARENTS

It is essential to remember that people who acted poorly as spouses can still be excellent, or at least average, parents. Children do not need parents who are perfect. The pediatrician and psychoanalyst Donald Winnicott wrote about the idea of the "good-enough" parent. This means that a parent needs to be loving and attuned, but it is actually not helpful for a parent to be too attuned, and fulfill all of the child's needs, which precludes a child from learning to be independent and confident. Your co-parent does not have to be perfect—he or she only needs not to be emotionally, physically, or sexually abusive. It is in fact emotionally abusive to your child to set up a situation where her relationship with your co-parent is not honored and supported.

Even parents who are mentally ill or who have committed crimes and are in prison can still be loving parents who enrich a child's life. As long as a parent wants to give love to his or her child, it is the other parent's responsibility to foster this relationship. We will discuss these types of unique situations later in this chapter, in the sections on violence, mental illness, and co-parents who will not or cannot see their children.

Remember, as children grow older, they will replicate the patterns they learned at home with their peers and intimate partners. Children who are familiar with a good guy/bad guy or perpetrator/victim dynamic from their parents' interactions pre- and post-divorce will be subconsciously drawn to these patterns in their own lives, or will create them where they don't at first exist. Additionally, adult children may never fully respect or enjoy time with the parent that was subtly put down during their formative years. Another twist is that children often get along worse with a parent that they fear they resemble. A child with a mother that she has been led to perceive as "crazy" will denigrate this mother even more due to the fear of being "crazy" just like her. On the deepest level, children suffer from low self-esteem when they perceive that one parent is deeply flawed, because that parent is half of them.

If you realize that you have been badmouthing your co-parent and causing a rift to open up between your child and your co-parent, it is time to take a hard look at what you are stealing from your child. Not only is your child grieving a non-divorced family, but now he has learned that he has to hide or change his feelings about your co-parent in order to meet with your approval. This is crazy-making for children, and the way that they often resolve this mental anguish is to truly start believing that one parent is bad. Of course, this "solution" is a poor one, as it prevents the child from having a close and loving bond and also undermines his self-esteem. Jane's story is one example of how parental badmouthing can have devastating consequences.

Jane, a DrPsychMom.com reader, shares: Both of my parents and then their new mates badmouthed each other. My mother was probably the worst, and since I lived with her I heard more bashing from her than from my dad. I would see my father every third weekend and two weeks in the summer. I am in my late thirties now, so this was almost three decades ago.

My mother would say things like my dad is a cheapskate, and that he never even wanted custody of us. Then she would constantly complain about his new wife. She always put my dad down, saying that he was not a good person and making fun of him. Then things at my dad's house were always uncomfortable for me, too. Partially because I would remember what my mom said about them, and partially because my dad and his wife were relentless in attacking my mom.

In my dad's house, I was always hearing how fat my mom and her husband were. How stupid that they had two red cars, how they never saved any money, how we went to the emergency room too often, like for "a fart sideways." The distaste my dad's new wife had for my mom spilled over onto me, because she thought I was a "Mama's Girl." So then I was made fun of and put down as well.

Once my father divorced his second wife, my relationship with him got better. He didn't really talk about my mother so much after that. However, the damage was done. I always wondered why my dad didn't care for us, and why he was promiscuous when he was younger, things that I'd heard from my mother. I wondered why he even married my mom and had us.

I spent a long time hating my dad because of the nonsense that my mother said. Some of it was lies; some of it was just stupid. She would tell me how he made her take out the garbage when she was pregnant, like it was physical abuse, but I later realized it's not a big deal. She told me that when they got divorced he didn't even want my sister and me. Just all kinds of ridiculous hurtful things that really just hurt me in the long run.

How to Handle Your Child Badmouthing His Other Parent

It is completely normal for a child to complain about his parents. When you are happily married, it is a lot easier to take children's complaints in stride, and to see that they are developmentally appropriate ways for a child to assert his own needs or preferences, and to show that he is an independent entity. But when you're divorced, a child's complaints about you may seem like betrayals, and his complaints about his other parent may seem like confirmation of all of your own grievances. Therefore, your own emotions tend to cloud your ability to recognize normal, routine complaints voiced by your child about his other parent. Let's examine why many parents find it so difficult to handle their child's complaints about his other parent in a supportive and healthy way.

Obviously, divorce arises from a great deal of disappointment and conflict, and you likely have many criticisms of your co-parent's character and behavior, whether or not you voice these aloud. If your child alights on one of these issues in his own criticism of his other parent, it's very tempting to agree with your child, and even to feel relief that your child brought up this issue on her own, giving you apparent leeway to agree. You may think, "Well, I'm not badmouthing my co-parent if my child independently realizes that his dad is irresponsible! By agreeing, I'm showing my child that I empathize with her and I'm validating that what she thinks makes sense."

It's important to realize that there's a big difference between your child complaining about his other parent while you listen or offer neutral remark, and a situation where you add fuel to the fire by agreeing and even jump in with some "observations" of your own about your co-parent's behavior. Think about this as the difference between you complaining about your child's behavior in your own head, and someone else openly complaining about your child. Most people would feel hurt if someone else badmouthed their child even if the complaints were ones that the parent had already noticed. For example, while a mom may often complain to friends about her own kids being messy, it would be different if a teacher started a parent-teacher conference with complaints about the child's messiness. Even though she may agree, she would still likely feel put off and defensive. It is the same for your child; he feels that he can complain about his own parent, whom he loves, but it feels like an attack if you join in, particularly as you have already shown that you don't love your co-parent by divorcing.

It's also helpful to understand why children may bring up complaints about one parent to the other, in addition to just wanting to vent about a difference in perspective or frustration at not getting something they want from that parent. Your child may be testing you to see if you secretly want her to badmouth the other parent. Your child may be feeling that you are upset, and that a good way to cheer you up is to talk about your co-parent's limitations, or compare your co-parent unfavorably to you. It is very dangerous for your child to learn that a good way to get close to one loved one is to insult another loved one. This teaches that people cannot love multiple people or things, and the only way to love one is to reject another. This idea can cripple a child's ability to engage in fulfilling peer relationships, and to be able to accept that friends, or, later, intimate partners, can love other people (friends, parents, children) while still loving her.

Children may also voice complaints because they are anxious about fixing situations themselves. It is very harmful to the relationship between a parent and a child, whether divorced or still married, to have another parent act as a go-between, translating the child's requests and needs for the other parent. This dynamic does not allow the child to establish trusting and open communication with both parents, but only with the parent who acts as the "protector" against the other parent. It also means that the child learns that one parent is someone he needs protection from. And in general, your child does not learn that he himself is capable of expressing his needs assertively, finding solutions to his own problems, or working to find compromises. Of course, with young children or those who cannot express themselves well, it's a good idea to email or call your co-parent about what your child has told you, in an objective way, just reporting the facts and leaving out your negative interpretations. (We will discuss how to do this in the vignette involving four-year-old Julia, which follows the vignette about Kevin.)

The key to handling complaints about your co-parent is to stay in the present and empathize with and validate your child's feelings in the situation that he is describing to you (see Chapter 6). You must try to refrain from adding your own opinions about your co-parent, which destroys your ability to stay focused on what your child may be saying. Let's look at two ways to handle a situation where a teenager complains about his dad to his mom:

> *Kevin is 13 and comes home from a weekend at his dad's house complaining that there is never anything to eat there. His mother, Moira, finds herself becoming angry, remembering other instances of her co-parent's perceived irresponsibility throughout their marriage. She says, "Really? That's unbelievable. He knows you're coming on Thursdays. How is it possible that he can't plan ahead to have things in the fridge? I'm going to send you with sandwiches next time, I guess making a sandwich is beyond him. I am so sorry you're dealing with this."*

In this situation, Moira thinks she is empathizing, but she has not actually figured out what her son is feeling, and therefore has not addressed his emotion at all. She has jumped in with her own perspective, and even a solution that her son did not ask for, which makes her into the rescuer and her co-parent into the bad guy. She has allowed her own feelings about her co-parent to color her response to her child, which likely has had multiple negative consequences for Kevin.

First, he may feel ashamed of himself for opening up his dad to criticism from his mom. He also may feel like he is a baby who is unable to find solutions to problems on his own without his mother's intervention. He also may feel worse about his dad, because his mother has interpreted his dad's behavior as indicative of his dad forgetting to take care of him, which points to a lack of caring or investment. Lastly, Kevin has learned that a way to get solicitous caretaking behavior from his mom is to trash-talk his dad. Not one of these lessons will benefit Kevin and his relationship with either parent, his own self-image, or his current or future interpersonal interactions.

Let's see how this could have gone differently. After her son's complaint, Moira takes a deep breath and remembers to lead with empathy and validation.

Moira: "Boy, you sound annoyed."

Kevin: "Yeah, I was hungry all weekend."

Moira: "That's terrible. I know you get hungry a lot, especially lately!"

Kevin: "Yeah, Dad isn't used to how much I eat after basketball. They were surprised how much I ate at Chili's."

Moira: "Yeah, I bet."

Kevin: "I'm going to tell him I want to get bagels for the house so I can eat before we go to basketball."

By empathizing and not interpreting Kevin's remarks in the negative light of her own grievances, Moira facilitated many constructive outcomes. She empathized with Kevin's experience and validated how it makes sense that he would be annoyed if he was hungry. She allowed Kevin a non-judgmental and open space to speak more about this issue. She did not rush in and fix it for him, thereby allowing him to feel that he is smart and effective enough as a person to find a solution on his own.

Furthermore, by focusing only on Kevin's feelings, she was able to see that his dad did not actually do anything egregious. It appears that his household has a different norm, where the family eats later or eats in restaurants, and Kevin is acclimating to this norm. Kevin was not neglected, and there was no doubt in his mind that his father would respond well if he requested that bagels be purchased. And most importantly, Kevin was able to see that it is safe to mention his dad around his mom, even if he does not carefully pick and choose his words to portray his dad in the best possible light. By not jumping on the dad-bashing bandwagon, Moira allowed Kevin to feel relaxed and free in describing his life with his dad to his mother, and not feel trapped between the two.

Kevin is an older child, and he was able to find solutions to his own problems. What if he were younger or remained inconsolable even with his mother's empathy and validation? Let's take the case of Julia, a four-year-old who is upset that her mother doesn't let her sleep in a family bed anymore since her new partner moved in. Julia is complaining about this to her father, Jay, who is fairly irritated that his co-parent has allowed her boyfriend to move into her home within six months of the divorce.

We will see how he can keep his own feelings about the situation under wraps and focus solely on helping Julia process her emotions and come up with a solution.

Julia: "Mommy is mean since Ryan moved in. Now I sleep by myself and I never sleep, not the whole night."

Jay: "That must be really hard."

Julia: "I know. I cry."

Jay: "I'm so sorry."

Julia: "Mommy doesn't love me."

Jay: "I'm sorry you feel so bad. I know it seems like Mommy doesn't love you, but I know for a fact that she does."

Julia: "You know?"

Jay: "Yes, I know for sure that Mommy loves you."

Julia: "No."

Jay: "I have an idea, maybe you can tell Mommy how you feel about sleeping alone again and maybe she will have some good ideas to help."

Here, Jay is buffering the relationship between Julia and her mother, even though he himself feels angry about the new living situation. He is taking his own personal feelings out of the equation and allowing himself to realize that Julia's mother not wanting to bedshare with a four-year-old would be understandable even if her boyfriend had not moved in. His next step is to have a private phone call or email with Julia's mother, in which he shares that Julia is distressed. To have an even better effect, it would be useful for Jay to make use of his empathy and validation skills by saying something like, "I understand why you don't want Julia in your bed anymore, since she is getting big and also Ryan moved in. But Julia has told me that she's really upset and thinks you don't love her. I told her that you do love her. Just wanted to keep you in the loop." This approach will put Julia's mother in the most receptive possible frame of mind, and lead to the greatest probability that she responds empathically to her daughter's distress and reassures her of her love.

What if Your Child's Complaints Are More Severe?

There are times when a child's complaints are much more serious, or times when your co-parent has repeatedly been unreceptive to dealing with issues that you try to bring up empathically and non-attackingly. In these cases, it is important to have a face-to-face meeting with your co-parent to discuss what your child has been saying.

Let's say that your five-year-old says that her mother is mean and never gives her dinner anymore. You may feel a surge of anger and want to call your co-parent, demanding to know why she is so self-centered and irresponsible. But this would be catastrophic for your child's relationship with her mother and your relationship with your co-parent. After you keep calm and neutrally ask your child more about what she meant, you may believe that your child's version of events is unlikely. For example, there may be details that are impossible, or seem made-up from TV or stories, like that Mommy only feeds her gruel from the forest. If you suspect that your child is making up stories, first empathize and validate. For example, you could say, "Wow, that must be terrible. I wouldn't like gruel either."

Then, you can say something like, "Sometimes kids tell the truth about stuff like this and sometimes they make up stories, just kind of to see what will happen or when they are mad at their mommies. I believe you that this happened, but I also would not be mad at you if you ended up telling me that this didn't happen." This may be enough to let your child save face and retract a story that was said out of anger, right then or later on.

But don't diminish the feelings underlying your child's story. Either your child is actually mad at Mommy, or else she feels that the best way to get extra attention and love from you is to say something bad about Mommy. If a child continues to badmouth her other parent to you, think long and hard about whether you've indicated directly or indirectly that you would enjoy hearing a negative report about your co-parent. You can commit to saying nice things about your co-parent more frequently if your child has begun to consistently badmouth him or her to you. You can also empathize with your child's underlying feelings that would have provoked her to badmouth your co-parent, saying, "Sometimes kids are really mad at their mommies and daddies after a divorce. That's normal and I get it."

If your relationship with your co-parent is amicable, mutually respectful, and trusting, it may be useful to call your co-parent and tell him or her what your child said. Even if you believe that your child was willfully or unconsciously misinterpreting a situation out of anger, your co-parent needs to know what your child is saying so that he or she can handle this situation by repairing the rupture that led to your child being angry, or, at the very least, explaining it to her more clearly.

WHAT IF YOUR CO-PARENT IS "AT FAULT"?

Let's say that it is true that your co-parent is solely to blame for the dissolution of the marriage—by lying, cheating, or getting involved in illegal activities, possibly even leading to incarceration. Let's even imagine that we are in the unlikely situation that you had neither a direct nor an indirect contribution to any portion of the discord. Still, there is no benefit to telling this to your child, or to your child thinking of one parent as a terrible person.

While it is important that your child understand the basic reasons behind the divorce, this shouldn't be done in a way that makes your child hate or feel contempt for your co-parent. The short-term gratification of having your child know "the truth" (when "the truth" means that your co-parent is a "bad person") and be on your side is overshadowed by the long-term psychological consequences of your child feeling that half of his genetic material is tainted. Thinking of one parent as "bad" can also lead your child to believe that he should not have a relationship with this terrible parent, and that you are to be seen as a victim who requires protection.

I have many adult clients who are unable to form lasting and meaningful relationships with individuals of the gender of their "bad" divorced parent. Here is a common type of story:

A woman remembers her mother speaking disparagingly about her father throughout her childhood. Her mother's whole family vilified the child's father as well. The mother took on a "victim" role and the child became her emotional caretaker and resolved never to be hurt this way by a man. As an adult, this client married, but was never able to be vulnerable with her husband, whom she didn't trust on a deep level. She would retreat from him emotionally and physically. Eventually her husband, tired of proving his love, fell in love with another woman and left the marriage. The client took this as confirmation that she and her mother were right all along to never trust men. Only after a while in therapy did she realize that her own closed off behavior, stemming from distrust that she learned as a child, may have contributed to the dissolution of the marriage.

This story is, sadly, a very common example of what happens when a child learns from one parent that the other parent is a "bad" person, or wholly to blame for the divorce. Children generalize from that one "bad" parent to an entire gender, or sometimes even to people in general. If you don't want your child to struggle with trust, love, and intimacy as an adult, do your best now to make your divorce seem like an unfortunate consequence of two people not getting along well, rather than a crime involving a victim and a perpetrator.

VIOLENCE, ABUSE, MENTAL ILLNESS, AND OTHER UNIQUE CHALLENGES

There are other situations where it is even more difficult to know if or how you can maintain and nurture the relationship between your co-parent and your child. In instances where one parent suffers from addiction or mental illness, and/or has been emotionally, physically, or sexually abusive to your child, it can seem more obvious that the divorce, and its related problems, are primarily due to this parent's behavior. We will discuss these situations in depth, focusing on concrete ways to tell your child about the reasons for the divorce without vilifying your co-parent.

Domestic Violence

If your child has witnessed domestic violence at the hands of your co-parent, and you feel that your co-parent is abusive and volatile, it may seem dishonest to speak in a positive way about him or her to your child. You may feel tempted to say, "Thankfully, we are out of that terrible situation now, and you won't have to see that bad person anymore." However, not only is this not true (there will likely be contact if your co-parent fights for it, if only supervised visitation), but it also does not help your child make sense of the situation in the long term. For your child, fear and love are mixed together, and it's your job to help him make sense of this and move forward.

The most important thing for a child who has witnessed violence is to be able to reconcile two aspects of his parent: the angry and violent side and the loving side. Your task, even if you hate and/or fear your co-parent, is to facilitate your child's ability to love your co-parent no matter what. If you portray your co-parent as a monster, then your child is the child of a monster, and this will lead to terrible self-esteem issues for your child. Additionally, if you act as though your child would never want a relationship with such a vile person as your co-parent, this denies the reality that children are biologically wired to love their parents no matter what, and even a limited relationship, or one that exists mostly in the child's head, is much healthier than no relationship at all.

Here is an example of how to discuss domestic violence and supervised visitation with your child, explained by a father whose co-parent had untreated bipolar disorder:

> *"Mommy had a problem with getting very angry and throwing things. When she was that angry, she said things she may not have meant. You may have felt scared, which would make sense to me. The important thing to know is that Mommy always loves you, even when she gets mad. It is not okay to throw, hit, or punch when you're mad. People make mistakes and Mommy made the mistake of using her hands when she was mad. From now on, when you see Mommy, someone else will be there, too, like Grandma. If Mommy ever uses her hands or scares you again, please tell me. If you tell*

me, it does not mean that you don't love Mommy. But, grownups are supposed to know if other grownups scare kids, so they can fix the situation and stop the scary things from happening again."

If your child witnessed a great deal of domestic violence but misses and loves the violent parent, he may be angry with you for leaving the situation, since you usually seemed to act (in the child's mind) like the violence was acceptable. In this case, you can tell your child, "I am sorry that I kept you in a scary situation as long as I did. I finally realized that it was not good for you, me, or Mommy to be in the same house together. Now, Mommy can work on her problems with getting angry, and then things will be nicer when you and she see each other." Conversely, a child may be angry that you kept her in the situation for as long as you did. In this case, you can say, "I know I should have gotten you out of that situation sooner, and I made a mistake. I understand if you're mad and I'm sorry. Hopefully our situation will be better now."

There is also the possibility that you were the parent who engaged in domestic violence, or that you and your co-parent got into physical altercations in front of your child. In this case, it is important to immediately find a counselor so that you can work on your issues with anger management. You can then honestly tell your child:

> *"I am very sorry that you saw me hit* (or throw, push, etc.) *Mommy. I was very angry and I did something that was very wrong. I am working very hard on learning different things to do than hit when I am angry, like taking deep breaths* (or walking out of the room; there are many ways to deal with anger that are beyond the scope of this book but can be taught to you by a trained counselor). *I know that you were probably scared when you saw me hit Mommy, and I am sorry I scared you. No matter how I acted, I always loved you and I always will love you."*

If your child witnessed domestic violence, it is a good idea to have your child start seeing a psychologist who can evaluate him for post-traumatic stress disorder, anxiety, and depression. These may not be obvious to the untrained eye, as symptoms of disorders manifest very differently based upon children's ages and personalities.

Abuse

It is an even sadder situation when you and/or your co-parent abused your child. In this case, as I said about domestic violence, you must immediately get yourself and your child into counseling. Whether you or your co-parent engaged in the abuse, only a trained counselor can assess the abuse's impact on your child. This is non-negotiable, and if you can't afford counseling, ask your pediatrician or child protective services for referrals for providers who can see your child.

If your co-parent has abused your child, try your hardest not to vilify and denigrate your co-parent to your child. Nobody wakes up in the morning and says, "Today is the day when I will abuse my child." It is likely that your co-parent is troubled, emotionally unwell, and ashamed of his or her behavior, even if this is not stated openly. Make it clear to your child that the abuse was wrong and in no way his fault. Reassure your child that the abuse will not happen again.

But do not forget how emotionally vulnerable your child is after having been abused. Your child's first concern is often that his abusing parent is not in trouble and still loves him. Try to focus on saying that your co-parent loves your child but doesn't know how to show that love in the right way. For example, you could say:

> *"Daddy was wrong to touch your privates. You will never be alone with him in a way that he could do that again. I know that Daddy loves you a lot, but he also did a very bad thing. In his heart, he is a good guy, but his behavior to you was wrong. Grownups should not touch children's privates, ever. I understand if you feel like you love Daddy but are also mad or scared. Anything you feel about him is okay."*

If you can be empathic in this way, you are setting your child up for a much better psychological outcome than if you call Daddy a monster or an "abuser." This is the only daddy that your child will likely ever have, and your child may even express hatred toward him, but there are usually also ambivalence, fear, love, shame, and all sorts of competing emotions that make life difficult for your child. The best thing to do is get your child to a therapist, and also to say that it is okay to still love the abusive parent, although the abuse is not okay. If your child says he does not love his parent, that is okay, too.

If you were the abusive parent, take responsibility for what you did and apologize to your child. Say:

> *"I should never have hit you when I was upset. You did not deserve it and it was not your fault, no matter what I said at the time. I am learning other things to do when I am angry* (see previous example if you were the parent who perpetrated domestic violence). *I love you and I am very sorry for what I did."*

Remember that most children continue to love abusive parents. This is normal, and is not bad for your child, as long as your child also knows that the abuse was wrong and not an expression of love. So, your child needs to know that, for example, Mommy loves her and also that Mommy has an anger problem, or Daddy loves her but did a bad thing. Reinforce this perspective many times, and also add that it was not your child's fault that she was abused. In addition to your love and support, trained professionals will be able to guide your child to process the abuse that occurred. Find a therapist that your child likes and trusts so this healing work can begin as soon as possible.

Mental Illness and Addiction

Mental illness or addiction in one or both partners can often lead to marital conflict and divorce. Both of these issues can manifest themselves in various ways when parenting. Issues can range from a depressed or substance-abusing parent who does not engage much with a child; to a bipolar, borderline, or drug-addicted parent who experiences anger and rage on an unpredictable basis; to a parent that terrifies the family with psychotic breaks and delusions.

Whether you or your co-parent is the one with mental illness, you have likely experienced a great deal of shame over either having a mental disorder or exposing your child to this behavior in a co-parent. It's also likely that your child saw arguments over the substance abuse or mental illness issue, and exposing kids to marital conflict can be another source of shame for parents. This shame, if not processed, can lead to lasting anger and depression.

If it's your co-parent that suffers with untreated mental illness, you may be trying to get sole custody so that your child is not affected by your co-parent's erratic behavior. This can be another tremendous stressor. If the parent with these conditions is you, you need to find help as quickly as possibly, for your own sake and that of your children. Both medication and talk therapy together lead to the best outcomes for mental illness, and often talk therapy, medication, group meetings can work most effectively to help people with addictive behaviors, such as alcoholism and drug use. In fact, even if it's your co-parent who suffers from mental illness or addiction, it would be a good idea to seek counseling for yourself, to understand how to avoid getting into a dynamic like this with another disordered partner in the future.

No matter how unpredictable, volatile, or scary your or your co-parent's behavior has been in the past, every day is a new day and children forgive quickly. Younger children in particular are very forgiving and highly motivated to continue loving a parent even in the face of the most horrific or scary behavior. This is why it's essential not to demonize a co-parent with mental illness or one who struggles with addiction. And if the parent is you, do not engage in self-pity in front of your child, saying that you are a terrible person.

The most important thing to do as a parent in this situation is to be open and honest with your child at an appropriate developmental level. This can counteract the toxic shame that children from highly dysfunctional households experience on a daily basis. In homes where one or both co-parents suffer from mental illness or addiction, children learn, "Don't tell anyone what goes on in this house," whether this is stated explicitly or implicitly. This atmosphere of shame and secrecy is very toxic for children, and can be equally as psychologically damaging as any conflict or erratic behavior that has been witnessed.

Start being honest and direct about what you or your co-parent have been experiencing. To a young child, you can say something like:

"As you may have seen, sometimes Mommy gets very mad for no reason, and this is because there is something in her brain that makes her get very mad. There is medication she can take to help this and she will try to take it. I am sorry for the times you have been scared by Mommy yelling at you. Mommy loves you very much and when you see her, Grandma will be around to make sure that her yelling does not get too bad." (Insert your own contact or custody arrangement here.)

Another example, for an older child, is:

"I have realized that I am drinking too much alcohol and it's hard for me to stop. When I drink I usually go into my room and don't feel well, and that's why I don't come out and play or see you the next morning, because I feel sick after I drink. I am going to start getting help and working on how much I drink. I love you and I am sorry that I acted how I did."

Keep in mind that being open and apologizing for your past behavior (whether it is your own behavior or allowing your child to witness your co-parent's dysfunctional behavior) are essential to teaching your child that what you did was not normal and not okay. Both addiction and mental illness are highly heritable, and if your child has inherited your or your co-parent's predisposition to either one, you want to model an open, help-seeking way of dealing with these issues. This can break the cycle of untreated addiction or mental illness that is often passed from generation to generation.

In addition to changing how you talk about mental illness and addiction with your child, there are other ways to help your child process her experiences. First, your child needs to see a therapist in order to make sense of what she has witnessed. It is very helpful for children to have an objective, warm, supportive presence that can help them figure out what is normal and what is not, a difficult task for kids who grow up around untreated mental illness or addiction. Teenagers may want to attend support groups, such as Alateen, the teen version of Al-Anon, which is a support group for people whose loved ones suffer from addiction. Alateen even has meetings online, and can be very helpful for teens struggling with anger, depression, and other feelings surrounding a parent's substance abuse.

When Your Co-Parent Will Not or Cannot See Your Child

If your child has witnessed or experienced abuse by your co-parent, and you are trying to get sole custody, this is a unique situation. In this situation, it is appropriate to tell your child, for example, "Mommy had a problem with getting angry and hitting, and you will see her but live with me for now. She and I both love you very much and we are sorry that it has taken us this long to stop the hitting from happening anymore."

If you don't know when or if your child will see your co-parent again, either due to abuse, or a parent refusing to see a child for whatever reason (usually extreme anger and an attempt to punish the other parent, or mental illness), or if a parent is incarcerated, deployed, hospitalized, or a restraining order has been filed against the parent, you may feel confused about these very difficult and delicate situations. It is important to ensure that your child does not in any way feel as though it is her fault that the parent is absent. Tailor your explanation of why your co-parent is not around to the developmental level of your child. For example, for a four-year-old, you can say something like:

> *"I know that Daddy loves you very much, but he is not able to see you right now. He is not feeling well and it is best for him not to be around kids right now* (this is if a co-parent is rageful or has untreated mental illness and is refusing to see your child). *Maybe you can draw pictures or write letters to Daddy whenever you miss him and keep them in a special book. Then maybe one day you will be able to show them to him."*

You can also make a little photo book of the child with your co-parent that your child can look at whenever she wants.

Children of any age may be very angry at a parent that they can't see, even if it's because the parent is sick or imprisoned. Make sure to use your empathy skills to tell your child that these feelings are completely normal and okay. Reaffirm that your co-parent loves your child very much and would be with your child if he or she could. (Even in situations where a parent has abandoned the child, this is still true; if your co-parent had the emotional capacity to parent your child, he or she would be doing so.)

Focus on keeping the child's memory of your co-parent alive and well. Mention the positive times that your child experienced with your co-parent. There is no point in directing your child's attention to the negative memories or dwelling on the reasons that the co-parent is not available. You need to honor your child's love of an absent co-parent. It's likely that your child will begin to idealize his absent parent, and this is normal. Do not try to disabuse your child of the notion that the parent is perfect. This is a healthy coping mechanism that allows your child to more effectively deal with the hole that the parent's absence leaves in his life.

POSITIVE REMARKS ABOUT YOUR CO-PARENT

Rather than just avoiding making negative remarks about your co-parent, get into the routine of making positive remarks. This may be difficult if you feel hostile toward your co-parent, but it's extremely important for your child's mental health and self-esteem. Remember, your co-parent has contributed 50 percent of your child's genetic material. Every time that you say something nice about your co-parent, it's like you are complimenting your child at her core. You can share positive memories that you have about your co-parent, and mention his or her special skills and talents, noting which the child has inherited. If nothing else, you can discuss how much your co-parent loves your child.

Key points from this chapter:

- Change your language: "co-parent" and "living with" versus "my ex" and "visits"

- Badmouthing a co-parent is toxic for your child, both in terms of his own self-image and his ability to have a relationship with his other parent

- Parental alienation must be dealt with as soon as it is perceived, so that a child can recover a relationship with his parent

- Don't use your kids as go-betweens or in any way make their lives more stressful because of your own inability to communicate respectfully with and about your co-parent

- Empathy and validation can stop you from responding with negativity toward your co-parent even when your child complains about him or her

- Even when violence, mental illness, or co-parent absence are involved, there are ways to handle these situations that can buffer your child from a negative psychological outcome

- Even in the worst-case scenario of a co-parent abusing your child, remain calm and do not bash or insult your co-parent

- Challenge yourself to get into a regular routine of making positive remarks about your co-parent

PART 2

How to Connect at Every Age and Stage

"Children need love, especially when they do not deserve it."
—Harold S. Hulbert

In the following chapters, we will discuss four different stages and the specific ways that divorce may affect children as toddlers/preschoolers, elementary schoolers, middle schoolers, and teenagers. Remember that no matter how old your child is, she still needs extra love, reassurance, and stability in the wake of a divorce. However, the ways that your child expresses and shows her love, and the ways that she wants to receive love, can differ based on her developmental stage.

CHAPTER 8

TODDLERS AND PRESCHOOLERS

Toddlers are in a unique stage, in between babies and children. They are testing limits and figuring out how to get along with others socially. Preschoolers are savvie, but still have difficulty with many abstract concepts, particularly in regard to time and non-literal language. If you say "next week," they may expect it to happen tomorrow. If you say, "I'll see you later" when you leave them for the weekend, they think they will see you later that night. Communicating with your toddler and preschooler about divorce will be difficult, but speaking in a very simple and straightforward way will help your child understand and process all the changes and emotions that he will experience.

COMMUNICATION POINTS WITH TODDLERS AND PRESCHOOLERS

There are four major points to address when discussing divorce-related issues with children this age:

Tell Them Everything That's Happening

Kids this young don't often know what questions to ask, so they live in a state of confusion and anxiety in the upheaval following a divorce.

For example, if you pick up your toddler later from daycare one day because you had a meeting with your mediator, your toddler may think that you have abandoned him. Be very direct about any changes that occur or are going to occur. In this case, a toddler or preschooler could be told, "Mommy is going to be late picking you up from school today because I have a meeting. I will be there when it gets dark. I will remind you and your teacher that I will be late. When I get you, we will come home and eat dinner." Even a two-year-old without many words will remember most of what you said. Make sure to enlist any other care providers in being extra careful about telling your child what's going on. In this situation you can also ask the daycare workers to remind your child that you'll be late.

Give Them Extra Love

No amount of cuddling, special one-on-one time, reading books, or playing pretend is too much for a child undergoing a stressful life change. See Chapter 14 for a list of special activities to do with small children to show them how much you love them, as well as a list of little ways to show your child you're thinking about her, for when you only have a few minutes or seconds to spare.

Make Positive Remarks about Your Co-parent Whenever Possible

As we discussed in Chapter 7, it is essential to make your child feel that both of his parents are equally deserving of love and respect. Even if you're filled with hostility toward your co-parent, don't fool yourself that not bringing him or her up is being supportive and respectful of your child's feelings. If your co-parent is never discussed in your home, your child will learn that talking about his other parent is not okay, and he will feel tense, awkward, and guilty when mentioning or even thinking about his other parent. Instead, make positive comments about your co-parent. Challenge yourself to do this at least one time per day. Examples can include: "Daddy is good at sports" or "Mommy loved to take pictures of you when you were a baby." You don't need to lie and say things you don't believe, but even a neutral remark in a warm tone is enough to show your child that it's okay if he thinks about and loves both parents, no matter which parent he is in front of at the moment.

Keep Control of Your Own Emotions

If you're sad or angry, that's okay, but keep your emotions at a mild to moderate level in front of children this age. Toddlers and preschoolers orbit around their parents like their parents are the sun. When the sun goes dark, it is terrifying. It's far better to put your child in front of the TV for an hour than to cry or scream in front of him. If you find yourself losing control, say, "Mommy is just having a bad day; it's not about you" and seek counseling so that you can work on ways to cope without scaring your small child.

REASSURING YOUR SMALL CHILD IN DIFFERENT SITUATIONS

There are some particularly stressful situations that will crop up frequently during and after your divorce. Here, I give you a template for how to reassure your toddler in each of these situations. Remember, you can say the same things every time a situation comes up, and you should. Don't worry about sounding repetitive. As you know, kids this age love to have their favorite books read to them over and over, play with their favorite toys repeatedly, and watch the same TV shows repetitively. Rituals are important to them and a source of comfort. Kids love to be able to predict what a parent will say, because it makes them feel safe and secure. So, the more you say these things, the more your child will remember them and internalize them, and eventually say them to himself when in need of reassurance. Modify these statements as you see fit, based on the age and developmental stage of your child, as well as your unique and personal relationship.

1. Living arrangements. "Mommy and Daddy both love you, but we are divorced so we will be living in two different places. You will have a home and toys at both of our houses."

2. The drop-off. "Have a great time with Daddy! You will see me Sunday. I'll miss you, but I know you'll have fun with Daddy! I love you!"

3. Your child acts out, tantrums, or expresses sadness or anger. "I know you feel sad (mad, frustrated, etc.) right now. Feeling sad is okay. I love you and I'm here for you if you want a hug."

4. Your child misses you, and is sad during a phone call or doesn't want to go to her other parent's house. "I know you'll miss me and I'll miss you, too. I am looking forward to hearing everything that you do and I can't wait to see you on Monday!"

Tantrums

Toddlers are notorious for throwing tantrums and fits when they do not get their way, or when they are tired, hungry, or frustrated, or seemingly for no reason at all. When you, the parent, are feeling stressed to the breaking point, a toddler's tantrum may feel like it will push you over the edge. First, before reacting, try to use your empathy skills from Chapter 6. For example, say, "I am sorry that you're so sad. It makes sense to me. I wish that you could have both of us in the same house, but we aren't living that way anymore. I love you forever and so does Mommy." Often, empathy and validation coupled with a hug can help your toddler or preschooler calm down.

In more severe tantrumming cases, there are many great books to help you manage tantrums, like *1-2-3 Magic: Effective Discipline for Children 2–12* by Thomas W. Phelan, PhD and *Parenting the Strong-Willed Child: The Clinically Proven Five-Week Program for Parents of Two-to-Six-Year-Olds* by Rex Forehand, PhD and Nicholas Long, PhD. The key is to be consistent and loving, and to be honest with your child about what you plan to do for discipline. This is why time-outs work so well—you are telling your child that she has two chances (with the time-out coming at the count of three) to stop an undesired behavior, or else she gets a time-out. It is direct, and it goes the same way every time. Children find this an easy system to learn and understand.

Many people instruct parents to ignore tantrums. The idea behind this is that the child will not find tantrumming to be useful or reinforcing if parents pay it no attention. I disagree with the premise behind this assumption, which is that a child is choosing to tantrum in order to obtain a desired result. While this may be part of it, more likely, your child is experiencing intense feelings outside of his control and is unable to stop himself from tantrumming. Therefore, realize that a tantrum may mean that your child needs more support rather than less in that moment. Furthermore, pretending your child is not crying on the floor in front of you is invalidating and crazy-making for your child (and can feel this way for parents, too).

However, if you offer your child a hug and use your empathy and validation skills, your child may still need another bit of time before he can calm down. Often, you are tapped out of emotional resources and time at this point and cannot devote another half hour to soothing your child. Therefore, if you've been empathic and kind, but the child continues to tantrum, you can say something like, "I have to go start dinner. If you feel better and want to come in and hang out with me, that would be nice." You can be empathic and also not stop your life activities for a child's tantrum.

DEALING WITH REGRESSION

A typical question about regression sounds something like this: "My daughter is four and we just told her last week that Daddy will be moving out. He has been gone for two days now. Since then, she has started to say she is the baby and use a baby voice. She even had her first potty accident in over a year. What is going on and how can I help her?"

When children are under stress or feel anxious, their behavior often regresses. You might have heard of or experienced this happening when a new baby sibling arrive. During a divorce, small children become anxious about all the unexpected change in their families, and are not sure who will take care of them. Children unconsciously think that if they act like babies, they will be more likely to get cared for. Additionally, babies are not expected to make any choices or act in ways that are too difficult for them, like choosing one parent's side over the other's. Any potty accidents or disrupted sleep could be related to a child's desire to be a cherished baby again, or it could be related to her increased level of anxiety immediately following the news of the divorce.

It's important to reassure your child that your love is as strong as ever, and hopefully your child's other parent will do the same. The news of your divorce undoubtedly came as a huge shock to your small child; there is no toddler or preschooler who can conceive of divorce as the result of even tremendous amounts of conflict. Therefore, a small child who is regressing may be feeling extremely confused and frightened.

Here are some things to tell your child, again and again:

- When, exactly, your child will next see each co-parent (if you don't know, try for when she will be able to talk to her other parent on the phone)
- That your child will have a home with each parent
- Whether her school and activities will remain the same
- That you and her co-parent will always love her, and will always be her mommy and daddy
- That you love your older child now as much as you did when she was a baby

Emphasize that divorce is nobody's fault, and explain, even if you already have, that Mommy and Daddy decided they don't want to live together anymore because they don't get along, but that parents and children never get divorced. You can also explain that your child is a big kid now, but you still love to cuddle and hug her just like you did when she was a baby.

Reassure your child that anything she is feeling now is fine, including sad or mad, and that you are here whenever she wants to tell you about what she feels. This would also be a good time to read a picture book about divorce with your child, which can help open up a discussion about divorce and your child's feelings.

If your child is exhibiting regression, allow her to continue in this "baby" phase for a while. When your child starts to feel more secure, this phase will pass. Avoid showing annoyance or irritation and try to accept that this is the way your child is dealing with her sadness and worry. Giving your child extra love, reassurance, cuddles, and one-on-one playtime at this time will make a world of difference in showing that your divorce will not change your loving relationship.

EMPATHY WITH A CHILD WHO IS NOT VERY VERBAL

It is often hard for parents to remember that kids frequently have to express themselves non-verbally. Even if they are very verbal for their ages, they may not have the words to express intense emotions. Therefore, you will have to try to translate what they are feeling based on how they are acting. Let's look at an example of a dad trying to deal with his five-year-old son acting out in ways that the dad can't understand.

> *"My five-year-old son Aidan has started shrieking for no reason, at home and at school. It is very hard for me to deal with him. I have enough on my plate without the kindergarten teacher looking at me like I'm some crappy divorced dad. I have no idea what my son is even thinking most of the time."*—Fred, 40

Here is how Fred can set the stage to empathize with his son:

Fred: "Aidan, I want to understand why you're shrieking at school. It seems like you must be upset about something." (Here, Fred is assuming that all behaviors have a logical reason. This makes it easier for him to understand his son, because instead of assuming that his son is acting out "for no reason," he is assuming there is a good reason and he just has to figure out what it is.)

Aidan: "No."

Fred: "I understand why you could be upset. Things have been tough with going back and forth between my house and Mommy's house. I get it."

Aidan: "No."

Fred: "Are you angry with me for some reason?" (Fred keeps on trying to see what Aidan's logical reason for being upset could be. This continues to show Aidan that his dad is really committed to understanding him, and so he begins to open up.)

Aidan: "No. I don't like it here because I don't have my stuff."

Fred: "You are upset because you don't have your stuff. I understand. What stuff do you want?"

Aidan: "My bear and my Xbox."

Fred: "I understand. You miss your bear and your Xbox. That makes sense to me. I like having my stuff with me where I live, too. Let's think of what we can do . . . Well, I don't know if we can take the Xbox, but I can make sure to remember to take your bear back and forth. Maybe we can get you a different game for here to play instead of the Xbox. I can put something cool on my iPad for you, too."

Aidan: "Okay."

Fred: "I love you, and if you are upset about something, I want you to come tell me, and try not to shriek and yell at school, okay?"

Aidan: "Yup."

Note that Fred went out on a limb here to guess that Aidan was upset about going back and forth between houses, and that Aidan could also be mad at him. He turned out to be partially right but not completely. Either way, he used empathy and tried to put himself in Aidan's position and guess what Aidan might be feeling. He did not judge Aidan, such as by saying, "Even if you're upset, shrieking is wrong." Also, he mirrored what Aidan said about not having any of his stuff, without getting defensive, even though Fred likely put a lot of time into making a nice space for Aidan with toys and personal effects. Instead, Fred set aside his own feelings, and empathized with how hard it would be to feel like you don't have any of your personal possessions. He validated his son's feelings, even saying that he would feel the same way in the same situation.

Although Fred did do some problem solving, this did not seem to strike his son as invalidating since his dad led with empathizing and understanding his perspective. Aidan may still feel sad and upset, and he will likely even still shriek, but more importantly than whether or not he shrieks, he feels heard, understood, and loved by his father.

Other kids in this situation may never tell their dads why they were shrieking, or even be aware of why they were shrieking, and that's okay, too. Don't interrogate your child. However, you can play detective and try little experiments of your own. If you reassure your child more, does he stop shrieking (or acting out in whatever way he acts out)? If you say nicer things about your co-parent, does this reduce your child's anxiety and thereby lead to reduced acting out? What about if you increase positive activities, like the ones suggested in Chapter 14? Whenever you're faced with a behavior issue in a small child, or a child of any age, try to add love in as many new ways as you can, and see what effect there is. Even if there is no effect at all, extra love is never wasted.

"I Would Still Love You" Game

Preschoolers and elementary schoolers need lots of open and constant reassurance that you still love them just as much as you ever did. One game that they may really enjoy is the "I would still love you" game. In this game, you tell your child that you would love him no matter what he did, and give him a funny example, like, "I would still love you even if you tied all my shoelaces together!" Your child can ask you more and more questions, which may be funny, or may be serious, depending on the child. The good thing about this game is that it can open up a conversation about whether parents ever stop loving kids, which may be a small child's fear after divorce. As we discussed in Chapter 2, a child may think that if you and his other parent stopped loving each other, the same could happen between you and him.

Some unexpected questions you might get are, "Would you still love me if I killed you?" or other violent questions like this. This does not indicate that your child hates you or is consumed with anger (although he may in fact be angry about the divorce) but rather that your child is really testing if you're telling the truth, and you would love him no matter what. Your reassurances are the key part of this game, and the longer it goes on, the more you can tell that your child is at a place where he needs to hear that your love for him is never-ending. If your child likes this game, you can read a picture book together that builds on this theme. It features a little Inuit girl asking her mother if she would still love her if she did various things, called *Mama, Do You Love Me?* by Barbara M. Joosse.

Key points from this chapter:

- Toddlers and preschoolers may be very anxious and confused about divorce

- Be honest and clear when communicating about what will happen logistically to your child

- Be direct and empathic when dealing with any behavior issues, such as regression or tantrums

- Reassurance and extra love are of paramount importance

CHAPTER 9

ELEMENTARY-SCHOOL KIDS

The central need for children in elementary school is to learn and to have fun. They are often very excited about going to school and participating in extracurricular activities. Peer relationships become much closer, with many children making best friends, and being part of close-knit groups. Children at this age are much less impulsive than preschoolers, and can understand much more of what is going on around them, including more about your divorce.

THE IMPORTANCE OF ROUTINE

Their parents' divorce can make it very difficult for children to focus on classwork, homework, and outside activities. Their schedules are often disrupted, and financial issues can arise that preclude their continued participation in valued activities. It's very important for kids to feel that they are being set up for success in school and other activities. If a child wants to do well but feels that this is impossible, for example because he does not have someone to help him with homework or to drive him to baseball practice, he may lose heart and just give up on achieving anything at all.

Moreover, if a child thinks that spending time with her parent is coming at the expense of other activities that are just as important to her, she will end up feeling resentful and angry. It's developmentally appropriate for a school-age child to prioritize friends and hobbies over time alone with a parent, and recognizing this may help parents take it less personally when a child wishes to keep her same schedule even if it means she misses out on time with a parent.

No parents, divorced or not, should always prioritize kids' needs over their own needs or the needs of the family as a whole. However, children of divorce have just had the rug pulled out from under them emotionally. The issue here isn't whether you "should" prioritize your kids' desire for consistency in routine, schools, activities, and friends, or whether it is "right." It is an issue of showing your child that even though he wasn't consulted about the divorce, his needs and desires still do matter, and his happiness is important to you and to his other parent.

Activities or Parent Time?

Ashley, 37, has been divorced for five years. She writes: "My eight-year-old son is really into soccer, and is mad whenever he has to miss a game to go to his dad's, which is two hours away. I wish he didn't have to miss his games, but I don't know what to tell him. I think time with his dad is important, too, and, even if I didn't, it's in the custody agreement."

———————

Dear Ashley, it's great that you are taking your son's complaints seriously and not just shutting him down when he gets angry about missing soccer. A number-one issue that adult children of divorce bring up is resentment over having to miss out on activities and peer socializing. Many kids of divorce feel like second-class citizens, and that their voices are not heard when discussing their needs or preferences. This leads to anger, resentment, and, when children are older, the possibility of rebellion and acting out.

It's important to realize what a good outlet soccer is for your son, and how lucky he is to have found something that he enjoys so much. He's at an age where it is very healthy and adaptive for him to become interested in a sport or other activity, and to greatly value the support and camaraderie of his coach and teammates. His involvement in this activity is also a protective buffer against the stress and negative feelings that come with the divorce.

If we use empathy to understand your son's point of view, not only did he lose the only family he knew, and not only does he have to split time between houses, but now his favorite activity is being stolen from him. Further, he may feel, correctly, that it will be harder for him to progress and succeed at soccer if he gets less game time and practice time than the other kids. Instead of doing what he loves, he is forced to hang out with his dad, a guy who, from your child's perspective, obviously doesn't understand what matters to his son. Wouldn't you be upset in this situation too?

Is it at all possible to sit down with your son's father, leading with your very admirable statement that you think time with him is important for your son, and discuss ways that your son could attend all of his soccer games and also see his dad? Could your co-parent drive down and attend the games, and have the weekend start at that point? Could you give your co-parent more time during the week during soccer season? Anything that you and your son's father do to help your son stay involved in soccer will be viewed by your son, both now and later in his life, as a meaningful way that you showed that his needs really do matter to you and to his dad.

GETTING A SCHOOL-AGE CHILD TO OPEN UP

Some children may not ask very many questions about the divorce, or may stop talking about it after the initial flurry of questions. It's not a bad thing for a child to be more private. Every child is different, with his own unique need for emotional and verbal expression. The best way to help this type of child cope with divorce is not to force him into long discussions with you about his feelings but rather, to make yourself open and available for talking (or other enjoyable bonding activities, as we discuss in Chapter 14). When your child comes home, or you pick him up from school or after-care, don't interrogate him with a steady stream of questions. Many parents have observed that kids respond to "How was school?" with "Fine," so if this happens to you, change tactics. Instead, ask a few specific and non-threatening questions designed to engage your child and lead to a conversation.

Here are some good examples of post-school conversation starters for kids this age:

- What was your favorite part of today?
- What did you play at recess?
- What did you think of the book you read in English? (Or any subject that interests you and your child.)
- What did [child's best friend] have for lunch?
- Did the teacher say anything funny today?
- Did anyone do anything cool in gym class?
- Did anyone do anything embarrassing or silly at school today?

There are also plenty of non-school-related conversations you can have with your elementary-school-age child. Your child will feel flattered if you ask her input on something or compliment her in a meaningful way. This can lead to a deeper conversation where your child is able to ask you anything she has been wondering about, or the conversation can be an end in itself, making you and your child feel more connected. Here are other conversation openers:

Compliments that draw your child out:

- That's awesome! How did you learn how to kick the ball that way? (Or any other skill that your child has.)

- You're great at _____. Were you always good or is it from practicing?

Comparisons between you and your child, where your child wins.

- I used to collect _____ as a kid. Is that cool or not cool? (Kids love to tell parents how they aren't cool. You could have a whole conversation that your child finds hilarious, just by focusing on things you do or used to do that aren't cool.)

- I never was good at _____. Do you think you would have been my friend?

Advice or requests for help, to make your child feel that his thoughts are valued:

- What's a good movie we could see sometime?

- Do you know any good songs I would like to listen to on my drive home?

- Can you explain [back story of any TV show or book series that your child likes]?

General "You're important to me" comments:

- Hey, I thought of you today when I did _____. (Kids feel important and special when they know a parent is thinking about them during the day. They otherwise assume that your day is so busy and you are so important that you never have time to think of them.)

- Today someone came into my office and I showed them some pictures of you and talked his ear off.
- I always think about that time that we _____. What's your favorite memory of us doing something fun?

Questions that engage your child are a great way to get her to open up more to you. In the future, she will know that she can talk to you about the most important things even in the smallest ways.

WAYS TO BRING UP FEELINGS WITHOUT ASKING

At this age, children are already learning that expressing their feelings may be dangerous; they may offend someone, their words may be used against them in some way, or they may feel vulnerable and embarrassed. That's why when you ask something like, "How are you feeling?" you usually are given a quick answer like "Fine!" Instead of asking your child questions that he is unlikely to answer directly, try some of these ways to get the ball rolling about feelings without putting your child on the spot.

"Sometimes" Phrases

"Sometimes people feel [sad or other feeling] and sometimes people feel [happy or other opposite feeling]. Even at the same time." This is a good way to open up a discussion with your child about his feelings on a particular matter without making him feel scrutinized. It also brings up the idea of ambivalence, which is very important for understanding emotions. Divorce brings up lots of intense emotions, many of which contradict each other. For example, a child may feel love and hate toward you at the same time. If you're honest with yourself, you may feel the same toward your child, particularly when he is being very difficult and you're feeling angry and frustrated. Teaching your child that ambivalent emotions are normal and acceptable will help your child understand that it isn't weird or crazy to feel both love and hate, joy and sadness, anxiety and anticipation, or any other set of seemingly opposing feelings.

Let's say you've noticed your child saying that she doesn't want to play with the neighbor kids anymore after she gets home. You wonder if this has to do with the divorce. You could say, "You know, when their parents get divorced, some kids feel like playing with their friends sometimes, and then other times they don't. Sometimes they feel both ways at once!" Your child is likely to respond with her own thoughts on the matter if you say this in a casual and offhand tone, while engaging in another activity.

In this example, let's say your child answered, "Well, probably some kids know a lot of divorced people's kids, and they aren't the only one." Instead of saying, "What do you mean? At least two of the kids on this street have divorced families!" you could say, "I get it. Some kids may feel embarrassed that their parents are divorcing, so they don't want to see their friends and talk about it."

Don't embarrass your child by trying to fix her problem immediately. Keep the conversation in the realm of "some kids," not your child specifically. Later that day would be a good time to ask your child if she might want to sit down and brainstorm ways to tell friends that her parents are divorcing. If your child says no, that's fine, don't push your problem solving on her. It is often enough for kids just to feel heard by a parent and have their emotions validated.

Use Pretend Play

Play therapists have long known that the best way to understand what a child is feeling is through unstructured play. Play make-believe with your child, letting him direct the activity. It may be evident how your child feels from how he plays. Some children directly replicate their perception of their family life when they play. It's not very difficult for a parent to understand a child's concerns or perspectives when observing the way that he plays. It's actually pretty easy, once you shift your perspective from "we're just playing" to "we're playing and my child is also showing me what he thinks of the world."

Let's say you're playing mother and baby with your four-year-old daughter. It's her turn to be the mommy, and she has the mother doll say, "I'm not sure when I'll be back tonight." Then she tells you, playing the child, to make your doll cry. One guess is that your child is anxious and would like to be reassured about her parents' stability and love. To address this, you can play back in a reassuring way. In this example, you could take the mother doll and say, "I'll be back at 9 P.M.! Even if you're sleeping, I'll give you a big kiss on the forehead and then I'll see you in the morning." Or, better yet, you can ask your daughter what the mother doll should say to make the baby feel better. Use the insights that you get from pretend play in your life with your child. Continuing with this example, the next time you go out you can make sure to focus on telling your child when you'll be back, and reassuring her that you will always be back, and that you always think about her when you're out, no matter what you're doing.

Share Your Past Experiences

"I used to feel . . . when I was your age, too." Kids don't like being compared negatively to a parent when the parent was their age, but they love hearing stories in which a parent had some kind of insecurity that the child also has. Even if your own parents were stable and happy, it would be very helpful to think about a time when you felt whatever it is that you intuit your child may be feeling. You'll remember that this is a key part of empathy, from Chapter 6. So, if your child seems to be angry at your co-parent when he moves out of the house, try to remember any time you felt angry at a parent and acted out. Don't draw the link directly for your child, but just talk about how you felt at that time.

For example, you could say, "I remember one time my dad said he would take me to the circus and then he didn't. Boy, was I angry." Even if an older child says something cutting, like, "Well, your dad didn't leave you, did he?" this is still a way to get a conversation going. In this case, you could respond, "No, he didn't. You must be much, much angrier than I was. That makes sense to me." You have left your child feeling more validated, and also aware that you aren't perfect either, and that you experience negative emotions, too. This will make it likelier for your child to approach you in the future with other negative emotions that he wants to discuss.

Books

There are many great books about divorce for kids. For young kids, these include *Dinosaurs Get Divorced Too* by Jennifer Myers, *Two Homes* by Claire Masurel, and *Dinosaurs Divorce: A Guide for Changing Families* by Lauren Krasny Brown and Marc Brown. For older kids, some good ones are *My Parents Are Divorced Too: A Book for Kids by Kids* by Melanie, Annie, and Steven Ford, and *Mom's House, Dad's House for Kids: Feeling at Home in One Home or Two* by Isolina Ricci, PhD.

Reading these books with your child and asking her thoughts can be a good way to draw out your child's feelings. Ask your child what the books get right and wrong, or what her favorite or least favorite parts were. Even if your child doesn't want to engage about the books, just reading them will help your child feel less alone and realize that other kids share her experiences.

You Don't Always Need to Talk

Not all children process emotions verbally. Many kids like just spending time with a parent, engaging in a mutually enjoyable activity. No matter how upset a child may be, there is no benefit to forcing him to express himself in words. Males in particular bond mostly during shared activities, while females more often enjoy a heart-to-heart conversation, but whether your child likes conversation or not is based less on gender and more on his individual personality. If your child has never initiated a conversation about feelings before the divorce, it's unlikely he will do so after the divorce.

It puts a child on the spot to stare at him intently while asking him how he feels. An alternative to a designated conversation time is just scheduling some one-on-one time and seeing what, if any, conversation crops up naturally during a given activity. If your child has something to talk to you about, he will do so if you make yourself available to him and don't put pressure on him to have a conversation. But make sure that when you schedule an activity, it is honestly your focus. If your child thinks that you've only spent time with him in order to have some kind of deep conversation with him that you're "supposed" to have, he will be unable to enjoy the activity, and will feel a lot of pressure to respond in the "right" way. In Chapter 14, there are lists of fun activities that can help you bond with children of any age.

Even if your child is not very verbally expressive, it's still good for him to know that there is a designated daily time for you to check in about how he is doing. During this time, he can bring up any concerns he may have. This is called a "check-in," and is described in detail in Chapter 14.

Resilience or Avoidance?

Laura, 43, struggles with her daughter's silence: "My six-year-old daughter doesn't seem to be affected by the divorce at all, and she won't talk about it either. She still plays with her friends, she does well at school . . . I know she must be upset, but how can I open up communication with her?"

Dear Laura, the first possibility is that your daughter is resilient, and is actually not that distressed. If you kept her life fairly consistent post-divorce, and you and your co-parent are both engaged and attuned parents, your daughter may be adapting easily. Also, if there was a lot of fighting before the divorce and things have cooled down now that you and your co-parent aren't living together, your daughter may in fact be relieved. And of course, there is also the possibility that, as you fear, your child may be pretending to be coping better than she really is. This is a typical pattern among intuitive children, especially girls, who understand that their parents feel stressed, and don't want to add to their burden.

If you want to learn more about how your daughter is doing, and asking her directly doesn't seem to work, you can try one of the aforementioned techniques to indirectly open up communication. For example, tell her that some kids feel angry or sad when their parents divorce, and some are relieved. Wait to see what she thinks of this, and empathize with whatever she responds. You could also share what you would have felt like as a child, or what you did feel like if your parents actually did divorce or went through any marital conflict. For instance, you could say that you probably would have felt sad if your parents had divorced. This could make your daughter feel more secure in expressing this emotion to you if she feels it. Remember that children are sensitive to being compared to you unfavorably, so make sure that you do not add in anything like, "I would have been sad, but I would have dealt with it." The goal is to empathize, not to covertly tell your child how to behave more adaptively. You could also read books with her about divorce and ask what she thinks.

Try some of these techniques over a period of a couple of weeks, and if your daughter doesn't seem to have much interest in opening up more about her feelings, you can feel safe in concluding that she is either coping well or her coping strategy of choice right now is to throw herself into school and other fun things, which is a pretty adaptive strategy for a child. Don't push her and make her anxious that she is not giving you what you seem to want to hear. The worst-case scenario would be for her to make up some negative emotions that she isn't feeling in order to appease you; she would both feel unknown and misunderstood by you and might even end up convincing herself to feel bad. Just make sure that you continue to make yourself warmly available to your daughter every day even for a few minutes, and you will increase the likelihood that, if she does have any negative issues or need any support in the future, she will come to you.

HELP YOUR CHILD FIT IN

While it's very important to spend time with your child, it is equally as important to allow your child to feel a kinship with peers. Children of divorce may feel more self-conscious and "different" due to having a family structure that is uncommon among their friends. Therefore, it's important for children in divorced families to know what the other kids are talking about at school, whether this is a TV show, a new accessory or extremely popular toy, or the opening of a new kid-themed store or restaurant in your area.

While some parents worry that an early focus on fitting in will set their child up to be an unthinking conformist later in life, nothing could be further from the truth. The only way for your child to become confident enough to think for himself in later life is to have a background of basic confidence from being able to fit in at a young age. Independent thinkers are not created by parents who make a child feel that he sticks out like a sore thumb. And biologically speaking, your child's drive to fit in is innate; all animals need to be part of a group or they are exposed to danger and predators.

Honor your child's need to fit in by helping him, and not minimizing his natural desire to be part of his culture and society. Try to avoid being excessively rigid about screen time or about any other rules that may potentially cut your child off from knowing what everyone else is talking about. This may mean letting him see movies or TV shows, or buying your child a kind of toy or whatever the latest fad may be. You don't have to breach your own morals and let your child do things you're vehemently opposed to, but try to be flexible and empathic.

Key points from this chapter:

- Kids thrive on routines that allow them to focus on learning and having fun

- There are many ways to initiate positive conversations with your school-age kids about divorce or any other difficult topic

- Don't force conversations or put your child on the spot

- Understand and honor your child's need to fit in with his peer group

CHAPTER 10

MIDDLE-SCHOOL KIDS

Preteens, or tweens, are in a very unique developmental stage. They are going through puberty, and their bodies and hormones are changing. Their emotions are extremely volatile—they are sensitive about what they look like, who likes them, and how well they do in various aspects of life, like school and extracurriculars. They may not want to be seen with you or to talk to you as much as they did a few short months before, but you and their other parent still play an enormous and influential role in their lives.

Some experts believe that the preteen years are the hardest age for children to go through their parents' divorce. Middle schoolers understand a lot of what's going on, much more than elementary-school-age kids, but they still may have unrealistic assumptions about the divorce, such as that you and your co-parent are going to reconcile, that you'll never date again, or that their financial situation and their activities will remain completely unchanged. Preteens also find it difficult to self-regulate in the face of overwhelming emotions, like sadness, anger, confusion, loneliness, and guilt. They often withdraw, giving you terse or one-word answers, or else lash out with rudeness and anger. This can be demoralizing and even angering for parents, who are naturally worried about and interested in their children, and receive nasty and rude responses to the gentlest and warmest questions.

Don't let your preteens' rudeness or detachment mislead you into underestimating how much they need you. However, at this stage, you may have a more hands-off role, where you allow their own developing identities, peer relationships, and priorities to take center stage rather than spending time with you. The key is a balance between making yourself available for connection and not intruding or preventing your child from creating his own identity.

Son Has Withdrawn and Won't See a Counselor

Ally, 37, writes: "My son hardly wants to do anything anymore. In the three months since his dad moved out, all he does is play video games. Honestly, he has put on a lot of weight, too, from just sitting around and eating. He refuses to see a therapist and he certainly won't talk to me. I try to ask how he's feeling and if he'd like me to drive him to a friend's house or enroll him in soccer this season, and all he says is 'no' or 'whatever.' He doesn't want to visit his dad either, and I don't push him. I'm trying to let him heal in his own way, but I'm scared that I am doing the wrong things."

Dear Ally, this is obviously a frustrating and scary situation. It sounds like your son is having some symptoms of depression. This can show up as lack of interest and enjoyment in activities, lack of energy, and apathy. I believe that this situation warrants you overriding your son's refusal to see a therapist. When your son refuses to see a therapist, he is speaking from a place of sadness and anxiety—he has no idea what it would be like to see a therapist, and assumes it would be awkward, painful, or useless. When your son is an adult, though, he may wonder why you didn't push him to see someone who could have helped him at this critical point.

However, I don't recommend that you wrestle him into the car and force him to sit in a therapist's office against his will. Instead, you and his dad may find it useful to have a sit-down meeting where you both express your own feelings of concern in an honest and loving way. Apologize for the impact of the divorce, and see if your son wants to share any of his feelings about how his life has changed. Use mirroring, curiosity, empathy, and validation from previous chapters to respond to anything that your son offers, on the off chance that he does share his feelings. Tell your son that it's not your intention to hurt him in any way, and it's because you love him and you're worried about him that you are bringing him to see a therapist who can help him cope in better ways.

Give your son various options for therapists so that he feels invested in the process and he feels a sense of agency, rather than just being pushed around by you and his dad (which may be how the divorce made him feel). For example, ask if he would rather see a male or a female counselor, and if he minds seeing someone in your neighborhood or if he'd like the privacy of driving to a neighboring town.

In addition to this, encourage your son openly, and in front of his dad, to resume spending time with him. And in the same vein, if you have any type of cordial relationship, encourage your co-parent to keep pushing for this time. While I believe that time with parents is not necessarily always more important than other social activities and socializing, your son is not doing anything else positive on the weekends, anyway. He needs to see that his dad and you are both concerned for him and want him to spend time with both parents.

Sometimes kids refuse to see one parent because they fear upsetting the other; you have to be clear that you want him to see his dad and that you don't in any way find this offensive or aversive. Other times, kids refuse to see one parent to test the other parent, to see if they love them enough to force them to visit. This may be what's happening here; despite your best efforts, your son may feel that nobody cares about him, so he has stopped caring about himself. Show him that you love him with your proactive, loving, and firm actions, not just with your words.

SOCIAL LIVES OF PRETEENS

Preteens spend a lot of time with friends. Although most aren't dating yet, they become increasingly focused on romantic and sexual issues over the course of their preadolescent years. Middle schoolers are very focused on fitting in with their peers, and maintaining or increasing their social standing. This might manifest in embarrassment about parental conflict and divorce, and preoccupation with being able to continue their same social and extracurricular activities so that nobody knows that their circumstances have changed. Some kids want to tell their friends right away about the divorce, and others, more likely males or children who are not big on verbal expressions of emotion, may not tell many friends at all, at least at first.

Right and Wrong

Preteens are beginning to think about issues of "right" and "wrong," and are focused on what's "fair" even more than younger kids are. They engage in black-and-white thinking, where there are clear courses of action in every situation, with a lot of "shoulds," like, "My teacher should have given us two days to study for the quiz and not one. She is awful and unfair." Preteens may become focused on deciding who was "wrong" and "caused" the divorce, and may pepper you with questions about specifics of the marital issues. This is particularly difficult to handle if you feel that your co-parent is to blame, but it's never appropriate to tell a child that his parent caused the divorce unilaterally.

Even if there was an affair, and a child this age is old enough to possibly sense this or to have made sense of overheard arguments about it, the best approach is to say, "There were many issues in the marriage, and we worked hard to fix them, but it didn't work out." If a child this age asks you a specific question, such as, "Did you/did Mom have an affair?" do not lie to her face. As adults, children remember instances of parents lying to them, and resent their parents deeply for being dishonest in this way. Instead, say something like, "Yes, I/she did, and it was a mistake. It was because there were problems in the marriage. It was not the only problem."

Black-and-White Thinking

If you yourself are engaging in black-and-white thinking, you'll notice that your feelings are very extreme, especially about sensitive topics. Another term for black-and-white thinking is *dichotomous thinking*, because things are either one way or the other way, nothing in between. Use of the words *always* and *never* is a clue that your thinking has become too black and white.

Some examples of black-and-white thinking are:

- "My ex is a complete jerk and I hate him."
- "There was never a moment when I felt connected to my ex-wife. The whole marriage was a sham."
- "Either my kid comes and sees me every single weekend or else I am failing as a parent. Therefore, even for peer activities or sports games, there is no exception."
- "If he can't follow my rules on his weekends, it means he has zero respect for me as a parent."

Black-and-white thinking does not allow you take the nuances of situations into account, or to realize how your own behavior may be affecting conflicts. There is usually a perpetrator and a victim when you think this way, and this is an unhelpful, angering, and depressing way to view life. Your child will learn this type of viewpoint from you, and it will make it hard for him to maintain close, healthy relationships with both you and his other parent, because one of you will have to be "right" and one "wrong."

If you find yourself engaging in a great deal of "always" and "never" thinking, it would be very useful to speak with a therapist. This way, you can learn to see shades of gray, and to guide your preteen child to think about the divorce in a less rigid, more adaptive way.

PASSING ON YOUR WORLDVIEW

Children of this age are learning about ethics and morality, and your divorce can serve as an (unwanted, but no less meaningful) opportunity to pass on your perspectives on major life issues. For example, in *The Unexpected Legacy of Divorce: A 25 Year Landmark Study* (2000), a son vividly recalls a conversation with his father about persevering through marital conflict that shaped his view about marriage for the rest of his adult life. You can discuss many topics with your preteen child, as long as you make sure not to get into developmentally inappropriate specifics. Your thoughts on marriage, divorce, love, commitment, perseverance, hope, and self-reliance are all likely at the forefront of your mind much of the time. Your preteen is grappling with these issues as well.

If your child asks you about any issue like this, don't shy away from the topic. Try to answer openly and honestly, and, most importantly, do not lecture your child, but rather ask what she thinks about the topic as well. Your preteen's insights about these issues may amaze you, and can lead to a discussion that shapes her perspective on life.

Your preteen also needs a great deal of reassurance that she was and still is loved and wanted, even if the marriage didn't work out. Children of this age are old enough to realize that, if not for them, parents likely would not have stayed together for as long as they did and this can make them feel guilty or ashamed of their own existence. Just because your preteen may be less emotionally open now, and may not even respond to your "I love yous" is no reason that you should not keep trying to express your love, verbally and non-verbally. In fact, your preteen is likely desperate for these expressions of love and comfort but finds it hard to ask for them without seeming like a "baby."

How to Talk to Your Preteen about Relationships

Sometimes divorced parents are so raw and battered by the stressors of their divorce that they pass on a very negative view of relationships to their children. Specifically, they make comments that indicate that romantic partners, or sometimes an entire gender, cannot be trusted. Some divorced parents say things like, "Always watch out for yourself because men can't be trusted" or "Women are done with you once your bank account runs low."

Try to focus on the type of relationship that you want for your child in the future. If your child views romantic relationships as sources of inevitable disappointment, this self-fulfilling prophecy will make it much more likely for your child to be subconsciously drawn to partners who confirm this bias. Pre-adolescence is when children first start to view themselves as romantic and sexual beings, and it is key that they have positive thoughts about relationships if you want them to have functional relationships one day.

Sometimes your children develop negative views of marriage and relationships on their own, merely from watching the divorce play out. However, with some effort, you can change or at least challenge these beliefs and promote a more trusting and positive worldview. For example, Kara's ten-year-old son, Jameson, said offhandedly, "I'm never going to get married." Kara's heart sank, because she was sure this meant that he was irreparably damaged by the divorce and would never be able to trust an intimate partner. Instead of rushing to invalidate his thoughts, and say "That's not true; when you meet the right girl, you will," which was her first reflex, she tried to stop and empathize with and validate his emotions. Here is how this conversation went:

Kara: "You don't want to get married, huh? I can understand that."

Jameson: "Why? Do you wish you never did?"

Kara: "Never. If I didn't get married, I wouldn't have had you. Also, I had many good times with your dad. I believe in marriage."

Jameson: "Well, you didn't have enough good times to stay married. If you didn't have me, you could have left sooner."

Kara: "I think of it more like, the best part of my marriage was having you, and that's why I don't regret it. I can see why you'd be soured on marriage right now, though. This has all been tough on you."

Jameson: "It would be easier if you never got married."

Kara: "It's your choice whether you want to get married, but I want you to know that many marriages work. Mine didn't, but it doesn't have to be the same for you. One day maybe I'll be in a better relationship for me. Anyway, I love you and I'm glad I had you, even if my marriage didn't last."

Kara was able to use empathy and validation to make her son feel heard, and to get to the feelings behind his initial statement, which were fears that his birth was a mistake, and that his existence had made his mother's life worse. She was able to address this fear in a warm and reassuring way, while also telling Jameson her thoughts on marriage, which may stay with him for his whole life.

How to Talk to Your Preteen about Sex

Middle school is a great time to start talking to your child openly about sex. This is the time when you can have a great impact on your child's perception of sex and relationships by portraying intimacy in a positive light. This is also a good time to figure out how to best convey your feelings about sex to your child. In addition to focusing on having sex only when you feel ready and with a partner you trust, be sure to emphasize that sex is a wonderful way to express love between two adults.

Many divorced parents feel cynical and disillusioned about sex, and portray it in a negative light to their children, either consciously or unconsciously. Do not poison your child against the idea of sex as a healthy expression of affection within a relationship, no matter what your own experiences have been. Do not act as though people with high sex drives (which includes most hormonally-charged adolescents and pre-adolescents) are contemptible or disgusting. Also, do not portray males as sexual predators or only focused on sex—a worldview that will diminish your sons' self esteem and make your daughters terrified of male-female relationships. Overall, any negativity about sex that a child overhears from a parent decreases his chances for a successful long-term relationship as an adult. For more on the topic of sex, read Chapter 12.

BALANCING TIME TOGETHER WITH TIME APART

Middle schoolers start spending a lot more time away from parents than they ever did before. Kids go to more parties, hang out with friends all the time, get more involved in afterschool and weekend sports and extracurricular activities, and frequently sleep over at one another's houses or go to sleepaway camps or on trips with their teams or other organizations. This unsupervised time is necessary for your child's burgeoning independence and it's developmentally normal for your preteen to want to spend what seems like a lot of time away from you. Your child is developing an identity separate from that of being your child, and deciding who to be as a student, friend, teammate, and even future romantic partner.

Children of divorce often feel conflicted about spending time doing what their peers are doing on evenings or weekends. Going to the movies with a group of friends may seem to come at the expense of spending time with Dad on Sundays. Try to make it easy for your child to still have an active social life and to participate in whatever activities he enjoys. Don't guilt-trip your child about spending too much time away from you, but also don't allow too much time to elapse between visits; kids want their parents to want to spend time with them.

THE IMPORTANCE OF EMPATHY

Parents often tend to minimize preteens' social concerns, which can lead to major arguments. Empathy is the best approach to parenting a preteen. Although middle schoolers' concerns about their looks, their friends, or fitting in may seem minimal or silly to you, they do not feel this way to the children experiencing them. Additionally, it can be hard to be empathic with a person who seems as self-centered as your preteen. However, keep in mind that it is completely normal for these years to be the start of a fairly narcissistic time in your child's life. He may also feel exposed and vulnerable very frequently. If your preteen feels mocked or dismissed by you, this can sabotage your relationship. Make sure to take your middle schooler's concerns and worries as seriously as you can, and treat your child with the respect that you would want him to show you.

Key points from this chapter:

- Preteens are very focused on social concerns

- It is normal for preteens to want to spend time away from the family, with friends and while doing other extracurricular activities

- Now is an ideal time to teach your child positive lessons about relationships and sexuality

- Your preteen still needs lots of love and reassurance, but not as much physical time spent together

- Respect and empathize with your child's concerns, even if they seem unimportant or self-involved

CHAPTER 11

HIGH-SCHOOL KIDS

Many adults idealize their teenage years, and forget the stress, heartbreak, and emotional ups and downs of this stage. It does not take too long before parents of teenagers realize that these years may be harder on the family than any previous stage of child development, including the sleep-deprived newborn stage and the tantrumming toddler years. Marital satisfaction bottoms out when kids are teens, as Daniel Gilbert discusses in *Stumbling on Happiness*, because this is such a tough stage to parent.

Why are teenagers so difficult, volatile, and unpredictable? High-school-age kids are figuring out who they are and who they want to be, which includes their strengths and weaknesses, their values and goals, and their place in the world. Their hormones are racing, and their risk-taking behaviors are at a lifetime high. This explains teenagers' tendency toward reckless driving, dramatic relationships with friends and romantic partners, unprotected sex, and overall poor decision making. Teenagers also engage in dangerous drinking and drug use, with 41 percent of high schoolers using alcohol and 27.2 percent using illicit drugs, according to the 2014 Monitoring the Future survey. Recent research shows that, while human bodies finish developing by the teen years, our brains continue growing through our early twenties. So, your teenage child's brain is not fully developed, and impulsivity, lack of forethought, and emotional peaks and valleys are the order of the day.

KIDS THESE DAYS

High school nowadays is a high-pressure environment for many kids. They have a great deal of schoolwork (far more than most parents did at that age), they have many extracurricular activities that shape their identity and self-esteem, and they are worried about the looming specter of college applications. On top of this, teenagers are figuring out their social personae, and place a great deal of value on peer acceptance and approval. Most teenagers also start exploring possible romantic relationships, which may include a sexual component. Teens want desperately to fit in, and anything that makes them feel like a misfit will affect their self-esteem.

Furthermore, the teen years are a time of psychological and emotional turmoil for many. According to the National Institute of Mental Health, about 11 percent of adolescents are diagnosed with a depressive disorder by age 18, and 8 percent are diagnosed with an anxiety disorder. Eating disorders, including subclinical ones, affect 4.1 percent of teenagers, including both males and females. Eight percent of adolescents engage in self-harm behaviors, including cutting. Aside from the teenagers who are formally diagnosed with these disorders, there are also many more who suffer from low self-esteem, poor body image, and depressive and anxious tendencies who do not meet full criteria for the disorders or who never seek mental health treatment.

Teenagers are notoriously self-involved and dramatic, and can be very volatile in their interactions with parents, particularly when they feel they are being treated unfairly. They often seem to argue just for the sake of arguing, and are trying out their ability to reason logically with adults. But despite how much they criticize their parents, teenagers want to be guided, especially with important decisions. They just don't often express this desire very openly.

It can be difficult for parents to accept that their adolescent children may no longer wish to spend much time with them. Hanging out with peers or romantic partners often takes priority, as do hobbies and other extracurricular activities. Younger siblings may miss the company of their teenage siblings just as much as parents do. And when teenagers are home and not spending time with their friends, they still may seem unreachable. Privacy is very important to teenagers, who already feel self-conscious and want their alone time to think, sleep, text with friends, or anything else. Some teenagers spend hours trying on clothes in front of the mirror, writing in journals, or playing online games with others. This is all developmentally appropriate, although it may be difficult for other family members to adjust to this new normal. If you are unaware of what is normal and healthy in teenage development, you may make the mistake of being too strict or un-empathic with your teen, and thereby limiting his ability to trust you and maintain a positive connection with you.

Divorce and Adolescence

Many people wait to divorce until their kids are older, wanting to give their kids the benefits of a non-divorced family for their young childhood. And in some cases, the problems just keep mounting until the situation becomes untenable, even if a couple had previously explicitly or implicitly decided to wait to divorce until the kids were out of the home. Although parents might think that teenagers understand more of what's going on, and wouldn't be as surprised when their parents divorce, this is often not the case. In fact, teens may have become inured to marital conflict or distance over the years, and perceive it as the norm. Teenagers are also in a notoriously self-absorbed phase of life. They are focused on themselves and their developing identities. Realizing that one's parents were not actually happy together can come as a tremendous blow to one's sense of reality.

In *For Better or for Worse: Divorce Reconsidered,* E. Mavis Hetherington and John Kelly discuss that adolescents experience a lot more conflict with their mothers following a divorce. This makes sense, since they often spend much of their time with their mothers and may idealize their dads, with whom they may spend less daily time. It is important for moms and dads to realize that divorce is extremely hard on teens, and to try and balance the desire to remain close with your teen with the reality that she needs her own time to branch out and figure out who she is in the world. If a parent tries to keep too-close tabs on a teenager, or forces a teenager to abide by rules that are much more strict than those in her peers' families, rebellion is likely.

YOUR TEENAGER'S FOCUS ON FRIENDS AND ROMANTIC RELATIONSHIPS

When you don't see your children full-time, it can be very hard to deal with the fact that they prioritize their peers over spending time with you. It's also hard to figure out when to push your child to spend time at home and when to let friends and social activities take center stage. Another area of conflict is when you disapprove of your teenager's choice of friends, particularly if these friends are engaging in behaviors that you find risky or immoral, such as drug use, sex, vandalism, and so forth.

Another notorious conflict between parents and teens is in the area of romantic relationships and sexuality. Although this is a high-conflict area for most parents and adolescents, it may be particularly tense when teenagers' parents are divorcing. At this time, teenagers may feel particularly lonely and misunderstood by their parents, and a boyfriend or girlfriend may provide emotional support and a sense of belonging. Parents need to understand how important relationships are to teenagers and prepare themselves for how to handle conflicts that arise over romantic relationships.

Research indicates that half of all teens report having dated and close to a third report having been in a serious relationship. Furthermore, many teens spend more time with their romantic partners than with their friends or family, and think of their friends and their romantic partners as their two most important sources of emotional support. When their parents have an unhappy marriage, or when parents are divorcing, it's natural for teenagers to feel very anxious about their own capacity to have a functional, successful romantic relationship. Many adult children of divorced parents make it their life's work to create harmonious marriages and families in later life, to prove that they are capable of succeeding romantically where their parents failed. This is a healthy goal, even though it initially may stem from a place of insecurity.

It's healthy, normal, and developmentally appropriate for teenagers to have romantic relationships. In my experience as a therapist, teenagers who were sheltered and forbidden to have early romantic relationships often have a harder time developing necessary interpersonal and relationship skills in later life. Dating is like anything else—it takes practice. Prohibiting your child from having initial, exploratory relationships is the same as denying your child any other developmentally appropriate activity, like sports or peer relationships.

Furthermore, discouraging a teenager from having a boyfriend or girlfriend is usually a surefire way to create conflict. In cases of divorce, this is a particularly misguided idea. Teenage relationships can be very loving, and can make your child feel happy and stable in a time of insecurity and instability. Rather than giving or withholding "permission" to allow your teenager to embark on a relationship, it may be more helpful to view your role as a guide who is available to help your teenager make healthy romantic choices. You can be there in case your teen has any concerns about his relationship, and to gently advocate for positive and healthy choices about physical and emotional intimacy. However, if you preach to your teenager, he will quickly shut down and dismiss your perspective. Many teenagers will bluntly say that your viewpoint is unwelcome since your own marriage did not work out, which can lead to hurt feelings and escalated conflict.

Here is an example of how a conversation can quickly go south when a parent tries to bring up concerns about a teenager's friends or significant other:

Mary, 45, is anxious about her 16-year-old daughter Ellie's relationship with her boyfriend John. She feels that, over the past two months, Ellie's focus has shifted from school and sports to being "obsessed" with John. Here is how their conversation starts:

Ellie: "I'm seeing John tonight. Can you drive me?"

Mary: "Okay. I want to talk about how much you're hanging out with him, though."

Ellie: "Mom, I can't believe you. Why are you trying to ruin my relationship? This is the only good thing I have and of course you have to take it away."

Mary: "Who said take it away? You're being dramatic. I only think that maybe you need to focus on the SATs and your grades. John is fine for now, but you're not thinking long-term. What about college?"

Ellie: "Maybe I am thinking long-term. John is long-term for me. This is the only guy I have ever been in love with, and maybe there are things more important than work, but you wouldn't know."

Mary: "What's that supposed to mean? My job that pays for your clothes, and for this house that you live in? Maybe you can just stay home tonight with that attitude."

In less than three minutes, this conversation has escalated to threats, veiled insults, and a feeling of hopelessness on both sides. Neither Mary nor her daughter feels heard or understood. Let's see if there is a way that Mary can get this conversation back from the brink using skills we learned in Chapter 6, including owning her mistakes, apologizing, empathizing, and validating.

Mary: "Look, can I take back what I just said about you staying home tonight? I don't want to threaten you. I know you really care about John and I do like seeing you so happy. I know you think you may be with him long-term, and who knows, maybe you will."

Ellie: "I mean, I don't know if it's for sure. But I want to keep him in mind if I'm deciding about colleges."

Mary: "Okay, well, we can cross that bridge when we come to it. Personally, I am anxious that you won't concentrate on school because you're too invested in your relationship, so that makes me snap at you when we discuss this topic. I'm sorry. I want us to be able to talk openly about this."

Ellie: "Um, okay. It's okay. I love you . . . because you're still driving me, right?"

Ellie is joking around, so the tension has been broken. Mary got her point across even if Ellie didn't show signs of hearing it. Ellie softened and admitted to her mother that she is somewhat insecure about the relationship. This is a first step to being able to confide in her mother if the relationship starts to feel overwhelming or if there is conflict with John. Most importantly, Mary validated that John is important to Ellie, and did not punish her daughter's rudeness by stopping her from seeing him. This would have been a terrible mistake, as Ellie would likely have responded by becoming even more committed to John. This is a common Romeo and Juliet dynamic, where the relationship takes its strength from the number of people who are in opposition to it.

Instead of achieving a short-term goal of stopping Ellie from seeing John for one evening, Mary took a long-term perspective and showed her daughter that she values their relationship more than anything. When you take steps to repair the relationship and bring it back from the brink of a bad fight, this shows your teenager that you care more about her than about getting your agenda across.

If you have concerns about how much time your teenager is spending with friends or significant others, figure out what is at the root of your concern. Do you miss your child and want to spend time with him instead? Or are you worried about the influence of a specific person or group of peers? If you have specific concerns, share them with your child in an open and non-attacking way. If you and your adolescent can have an open exchange about peer relationships or intimate relationships, this is "winning the war." Stopping your child from seeing one person or a group of people is just "winning the battle," and can lead to decreased closeness and trust between you and your teenager long-term.

Teenagers and Sex

While the idea of teenage sexual activity scares and angers many parents, it's completely normal. The average age that teens first have sex is seventeen, and the majority of teenagers' first sexual experience is with a steady partner. This indicates that it's entirely appropriate for a teenager to be exploring sexuality, and is particularly safe within the context of a stable relationship, which by adolescent standards likely means monogamous for a few months.

However, do not just look the other way and allow your teenager to proceed entirely unsupervised into the world of relationships and sex.

Teenagers still need parental input and guidance about relationships and sexuality. Instead of preaching to your child and saying what you do and do not allow, try to ask your child about her thoughts on relationships and sex. If your child views you as open-minded and tolerant, she is far more likely to come to you with questions and confide about possible problems. Irrespective of whether your child openly states that she is planning to have sex, it is good practice to give your teenager information on birth control and how to protect against sexually transmitted diseases. This conversation is best to have in the preteen years, but you should repeat it when your child is actively starting to spend time with potential romantic interests.

Make sure that you don't scare your teenager away from sex by focusing exclusively on its downsides. While this could, in fact, deter some teens from experimenting, you may end up giving your teenager a negative view of intimate relationships overall. Many adults come into therapy with sexual issues because they grew up in families where sex was considered "bad" or "shameful." Some divorced parents also feel bitter about the role of sex in their marriage, particularly if a partner was sexually unfaithful. They express this point of view with sarcastic or diminishing comments about sex, either saying that it's unimportant or that it's an issue of contention within relationships.

If you make a point to discuss sex as a healthy and natural activity and an expression of love between committed partners, you will be doing your part to increase the likelihood that your child has a positive intimate relationship as an adult. Talk to your child about what it feels like to be ready for sex within the context of a committed relationship, and volunteer to take your child to get protection if your child decides to be intimate with a partner. The worst thing to do is leave your child with no options if he does decide to start having sex. This is what happens with abstinence-only education—kids still have sex but don't use protection. Therefore, research indicates that the best way to deal with your teenager's developing sexuality is to be open, accepting, and informative.

Some teenagers become promiscuous when their parents divorce. This could be due to decreased supervision, a desire to distract themselves from negative emotions, or even increased interest in sex from observing parents with their new partners (see Chapter 12). If you realize that your teenager is engaging in sexual activity with many new people, try not to become angry or start a huge fight. Instead, approach your teenager calmly and ask about what you have discovered (or suspect) with love and concern. Kissing or fooling around with many new people may not be a cause for concern as much as having intercourse or oral sex with a range of partners. If your teenager seems to be acting out in an uncontrolled, self-destructive way with sex, or in any other area, find your teenager a good therapist with whom he can discuss these issues.

ACTING OUT

It is terrifying for a parent to witness a child's behavior spiraling out of control. Whether this is with drug use, academic underachievement, an eating disorder, or anything else, it drives parents crazy to see a child seemingly self-sabotaging and having no way to get the child back on track. Unfortunately, many parental expressions of concern are heard by a teenager as humiliating criticism. This isn't just because teenagers can be dramatic (although they can be), but because many parents express themselves in ineffective ways. The following two examples show common issues parents have with teenagers, and ways to handle them.

He Won't Listen to Me Anymore

Carol, 42, is terrified that her 16-year-old son's behavior is spiraling out of control. She writes: "Ever since the divorce, my son is a different kid. He never used to be a partier, but now he's getting high all the time. I don't let him do it at home, but I know he's doing it with friends. I try to ground him, but he laughs in my face and tells me he'll do what he wants at school, anyway. He acts like he hates me. He idolizes his father, though, and of course Dad can do no wrong. He knows our son smokes pot and he doesn't care. I'm the only disciplinarian, just like before we divorced, but worse, because now he's away from me on the weekends and I have no idea what his dad is letting our son do."

———————————————

Dear Carol, this is certainly a difficult and scary situation. It seems like your son has lost respect for you in the aftermath of the divorce, and is painting his father as the good guy. I think the most important issue to deal with is your son's relationship with you. Sadly, there is not going to be much of a way to "fix" your son's behavior if your son feels angry toward you and contemptuous of your rules. As he points out himself, he can find ways around any rule that you give him. This is why conflict escalates so dramatically in some families with teenagers, to the point of sending children to military school or other extreme measures. It makes parents crazy with fear to realize that they literally cannot control their children. However, many times the behavior can be addressed more effectively by addressing the relationship rupture between the parents and the teenager.

In your case, I recommend that you sit down with your son and tell him that you love him and are sorry about how your relationship has gotten worse since the divorce. Apologize for anything that you yourself may have done that has contributed to the current state of affairs. For example, have you always been kind, patient, and warm? Of course not; no parent is perfect. Own your part in getting your relationship to where it is now. Ask your son with open curiosity how he feels about you and about the divorce. He may surprise you and tell you, and some things may be painful to hear. No matter what he says, you must show him that you can be trusted and will not lash back at him or be defensive. Truly attempt to empathize with him and validate his experiences, thoughts, and feelings. If he doesn't share any thoughts or feelings with you, tell him you will always be there if he wants to talk.

Overall, I recommend that you treat your son like the independent adult that he wishes he were. Take the pot smoking and all his other behaviors out of the equation for now and focus on building back your relationship with your son. Do fun activities together, or express your love in other ways (see Chapter 14). Focus on being emotionally present and not on criticizing your son or giving him unwanted advice. It's honestly better for him to fail out of school and have a loving relationship with you than to succeed academically and hate his mother, which will set him up for later difficulties with interpersonal relationships throughout his life. Your son can always get his GED, but neither of you will later be able to go back in time and repair his adolescent relationship with you.

Let's look at another example, of a dad whose daughter is angry with him and does not value their time together.

She Hates Me

Dan, 45, says: "I looked outside the marriage for emotional connection, and had a brief affair that my ex-wife discovered. I know it was wrong and it was a symptom of how disconnected and messed up our marriage was. We divorced six months ago. My relationship with my 15-year-old daughter remained strong until her mother told her that I cheated. Now my daughter hates me. She won't pick up the phone when I call and she doesn't return texts. She has told me that what I did ruined her mom's life. She tries to get out of seeing me on the weekends, but I insist that she comes. Is this making things worse? I just want her to know that no matter what happened between her mom and me, it doesn't impact who I am as a father. This is much worse because I'm not a big phone person and she won't agree to see me in person."

Dear Dan, this is a very difficult situation, and I can see why you're in pain. Teenagers have a very clear-cut idea of what is right and what is wrong. This black-and-white thinking is hurting you now; your daughter thinks you are all "bad," and she wants nothing to do with you. Her mother may also be saying other things about you; it's unclear if this is parental alienation (see Chapter 7) or if she was just explaining why she feels the marriage ended.

First of all, you need to get your daughter to agree to a face-to-face meeting. Drive out to the house or take her to a restaurant. Do whatever you have to do in order to get this meeting; as Richard Warshak writes in *Divorce Poison*, spending face-to-face time with your kids can prevent parental alienation from developing. Then, apologize to your daughter sincerely for your contribution in breaking up the family. It's essential to own your part in the marital problems and the divorce, and to tell your daughter that you regret having been dishonest. You can also assure your daughter that just because you were dishonest in this one regard does not mean that she can't trust you as a dad. Explain that you love her and nothing will ever change that. Especially if you are not a very verbally expressive guy, your daughter will value hearing you say these things, even if she doesn't admit it. Tell her that you love her and how sad you are to think about your relationship being jeopardized.

Next, tell your daughter that you love her but you don't want to force her to spend time with you that she doesn't enjoy. It's very important for teenagers to feel that their parents respect them and value their needs. But it's also important that they see that you don't easily capitulate when they try to get out of seeing you. Sometimes children test their divorced parents to see if their parents are checking off a box on the custody agreement or if they truly want to spend time with them. If you allow your daughter to get out of seeing you that easily, she may be secretly hurt and disappointed. Therefore, you have to balance your need to see her with her need to assert her own boundaries and needs.

In order to balance these two issues, try to work with your daughter to come up with compromises in terms of how and when you two will spend time together. Tell her that you know that it's important for her to have time with friends and time for schoolwork and hobbies, but time with you is necessary, too. Come up with a schedule for spending time together that she can agree to, and share it with your co-parent, who will hopefully be on board.

SUPERVISING TEENAGERS: A DELICATE BALANCE

Adolescence is a very important stage; it is when major decisions are made about college, when kids get their first jobs, and when they start dating. It's normal to want to protect your child from making painful mistakes, particularly if they are the same mistakes that you made when you were an adolescent yourself. For example, many parents realize that their teenagers' decisions about academics, romantic relationships, or peer interactions are not going to lead to successful outcomes. And some teenage mistakes seem so easy to fix, like breaking up with a partner that causes you pain, studying a week early for a test instead of cramming the night before, or going to bed earlier if you know you tend to oversleep in the morning.

It can be exciting and harrowing to watch high schoolers navigate increasingly challenging schoolwork, start new romantic and peer relationships, figure out who they are as people, and develop areas of interest and passion. When responding to the challenges of raising adolescents while in the midst of a stressful divorce, parents sometimes take one of two extreme paths. Some divorcing parents give their children too much space and leniency, while others become so invested in their teenagers' academic lives that they end up doing more harm than good. Let's explore the effects of each of these paths.

The Uninvolved Parent

Sometimes parents are so stressed or feel so unable to deal with each other that they abdicate the parent role, hoping that their teenage children are mature enough to deal with things entirely on their own.

Raising Myself

Haley, a DrPsychMom.com reader, shares her experience as a teenage child of divorce:

"I'm a grown child of divorce and I have many terrible memories from my parents' split. It happened just a couple of weeks before I started 9th grade, and a month before my 15th birthday. I was sad but mature enough to know that my parents had a terrible marriage and I felt that it probably was for the best.

However, soon after the divorce, my parents just stopped parenting me altogether, and my heart broke. I was essentially on my own. My parents didn't speak to each other, and when I needed anything (money, clothes, rides to school functions and sports practices) I had to negotiate between the two of them and usually ended up having to figure things out for myself.

I was unsupervised the majority of the time and took full advantage. My parents were so wrapped up in their own lives that they would often just sweep things under the rug instead of dealing with me. Every holiday was stressful because I never felt like I had a place to go. I always felt like a burden or an afterthought. This is no way to express how important it is for divorced parents to work together. No matter how difficult, it needs to be a priority. It took me years to forgive my mom for her behavior and I still haven't fully forgiven my dad.

I never wanted to get married or have a family of my own because of this fear (I was a serial dater and all around commitment-phobe until I was 25 and met my husband). It's now 20 years later and I'm married with two kids of my own. My marriage is rocky right now and divorce may very well be our next step. My heart is breaking again from the experience I had with my parents, and the fear that my children could end up feeling the way I did."

It is essential that parents do not delude themselves into thinking that their teenager is far more mature and adult than he really is. As we discussed in Chapter 3, a child should not be pushed into an adult role, whether this is playing confidante to a parent, acting as a parent to siblings, or even parenting himself. Your teenager is not a child anymore, but he is definitely not capable of fully supporting himself financially (although a part-time job is fine) or living an entirely independent life without supervision.

When teenagers believe that their parents don't care, they can turn to other outlets to distract them from their sadness and loneliness, such as too-intense romantic relationships, drugs, alcohol, and eating disorders. Whether or not you can be present at every game or school show, it's important that you attend some of them, and that you know about and ask about the rest. If you feel very overwhelmed and stretched for time, you can set up an online calendar and sit down with your teenager to input the most important activities for each week. Then you can try to get to as many as possible, or at least text your teenager to see how they went. Any involvement, no matter how limited, is better than nothing.

The Over-Involved Parent

On the other hand, it's necessary to realize that the teenage years are a time for your child to become independent, and to make necessary mistakes that she can learn from in the future. Many children whose parents micromanaged their schedules and deadlines and helped intensively with their school assignments all through high school come to college completely unprepared to manage their own lives. Such kids often fail out or decide to take a break from college and come home. They have no idea how to be self-reliant, because their parents did not give them increasing levels of independence over the course of their childhood and adolescence.

Many divorced parents throw themselves into parenting with new vigor, partially to compensate for any guilt about the divorce, and partially because there is no other relationship to focus on. While it's great to be present, your child will not thrive under a hovering, "helicopter-parent" approach. Additionally, your child may feel that the divorce has led to him being more mature than peers, and may particularly resent close monitoring that he feels is suffocating or befitting a much younger child.

Despite your best intentions, you are doing your child no favors by too-closely monitoring every aspect of his life and his decision making. This approach may end up stunting his ability to function on his own, by depleting his confidence in himself. If you don't think your teenager can succeed without your help, why would he think he can? And how would he ever develop the concrete skills he needs to succeed?

It's also useful to understand the true limits of your control. If you tell a child not to see a friend or a significant other, is this really going to stop your child from doing it? Many adults in therapy have shared that they learned how to be good liars because of the constrictions placed on them by their overly punitive parents. Furthermore, would it really be a positive for an adolescent to blindly adhere to whatever rules you set forth, even if she feels very strongly about something, such as seeing a significant other? If you want your child to be strong, independent, and confident as an adult, it's unlikely that this sort of person would emerge from a teenager that never deviates from rules that are perceived as unjust or arbitrary.

Research shows that authoritative parenting, which is empathic but firm, is better than authoritarian (overly strict) or permissive (overly lax) parenting. Authoritative parenting is when you set rules but allow your children to discuss them with you and communicate their own perspectives. If your child's position is logical, you can compromise or change the rules. This parenting style is correlated with kids who can think independently and negotiate with others, and who feel valued and respected. In contrast, permissive, overly lenient parenting leads to kids who act narcissistic and who can't follow rules, and authoritarian parenting can lead to kids who are rebellious or entirely dependent and unable to think for themselves.

Overall, it's always best to use empathy and understanding to truly put yourself in your teenager's shoes when deciding on rules and boundaries. Parents are frequently surprised at how mature their adolescent acts when he is in a situation with a great deal of responsibility, such as at a summer job. Often, if approached with respect and warmth, your adolescent can be enlisted to come up with rules that are compromises and that take both his desires and yours into account. Always try a warm and flexible approach and get firmer from there if need be. The goal is to raise a fully functioning, independent adult. If you start with firm and unyielding rules, you never get a chance to see if your child would have risen to the occasion if he was granted more independence from the get-go.

SCHOOLWORK

For divorcing or divorced parents, handling teenagers' schoolwork is often a major source of conflict. When kids are stressed, their academic performance can suffer greatly. This can be crazy-making for parents of high schoolers. Parents understand that grades at this point are critical to college acceptance. As you may have observed if you're in this position yourself, nagging your child about his grades rarely does much aside from create conflict and stress for everyone in the home. But it feels impossible and ethically remiss to just ignore your teen's poor academic performance and seemingly deliberate apathy toward schoolwork, standardized tests, and college admissions deadlines. So what are you to do?

Again, you will be mobilizing your skills of empathy and validation to communicate more effectively with your child. For example, telling your teenager that "grades count" and "colleges care about your grades" will not get you very far if your child does not care much about grades or college himself. Instead, try to ask your teenager about his own personal academic and career goals. If you are accepting of your child's life goals, then he will be more accepting of your input. This means that if your son wants to be a musician, it will do nothing positive for your relationship if you tell him how unlikely it is to succeed in this field. If you are supportive and nurturing of his dream, he may listen to you when you ask him to focus more on school.

Additionally, there is often conflict between co-parents about how to handle schoolwork. One parent is thought to be too laissez-faire, and the other is thought to be rigid and controlling. It is very tempting for each parent to blame the other for how a teenager mishandles his academic work, but please try to refrain from viewing your co-parent as the enemy. Also, teenagers often play co-parents against each other in this arena, saying that "Dad is more laid-back" or "Mom trusts me to do what I have to do." And some children also side with the stricter parent, saying "At least Mom cares."

It's best for both co-parents to sit down with their child individually and decide the limits of their involvement. Rules can be different at each house, and should be respected. For example, Dad may not view his role as an enforcer, particularly with an older adolescent, and may shy away from making sure that a teenager does her homework each night. Mom may require that a teenager show her completed assignments before going out for the evening. Unless your co-parent's behavior verges on abusive, e.g., not letting a teenager have a normal social life and instead forcing her to stay home on weekends and study, or having severe punishments for low grades, it is best to allow your co-parent to have his or her own rules in place for how to handle schoolwork. Also, make sure that you convey to your child that playing one parent against the other will not be tolerated.

As we just discussed, it's necessary to strike a balance between under-involvement and over-involvement. You need to know what your child is doing in school, but monitoring a teenager's every homework assignment is infantilizing and does not teach your child that you have faith or confidence in his ability to function on his own. After a certain point, it is your child's decision whether he will concentrate on school, apply to colleges, and investigate financial aid options. Although you can be present and available during these processes, and give advice to the best of your ability, it may be necessary to consciously take a step back if you realize that your involvement is leading to a lot of extra conflict between you and your child.

Pre-College Stress

College is a huge financial burden. Tuitions are higher now than they have ever been, and many intact, dual-income families are unable to pay for their children's college tuition. Often, this is a source of guilt and shame. In many cases, parents were given financial help by their own parents, and now are in no position to do so for their own kids.

This sense of guilt and shame grows exponentially when parents are divorced. Parents often feel like their divorce prevented them from reaching a financial place where they could afford to contribute to their children's college experience. Children often openly complain about their parents' inability to help them financially, particularly if their peers are receiving help and if they tried hard academically throughout their schooling. These complaints can be worse if children believe that one parent's selfishness or irresponsibility led to a lack of funding. For example, if a divorced dad remarried and bought a new house for himself and his new partner, his teenage child may think, and say, that this financial decision was unfair and led to less available money for college.

Money is a sensitive topic at the best of times, but discussing money openly with a possibly argumentative and attacking adolescent or young adult is even more stressful. Even though this may be difficult, openness and honesty are necessary if you want to have a reasonable and trust-inspiring conversation with your teenager. Teenagers often rise to the occasion; if you speak to them reasonably and openly, they often respond with maturity. Similarly, if you lead with empathy, they are likelier to be empathic toward you.

Difficult Talk about College Tuition

It is time for 17-year-old Tyler to apply to colleges. He is a great lacrosse player but does not know if he will receive an athletic scholarship. His mother, Anne, is a teacher and has not been able to set aside any savings since her divorce. She has been delaying having an honest conversation with Tyler about the limits of her possible financial help, in part because she is ashamed about how little she will be able to contribute, and in part because she is angry that her co-parent, a lawyer, has not volunteered to pay the tuition himself and is sticking to the amount specified in the child support agreement. Here is an example of a conversation where Anne uses honesty and empathy, and also refrains from badmouthing Tyler's dad.

Anne: "Hey Tyler, I really need to talk to you about colleges before you decide where to apply."

Tyler: "We've talked about it. UCLA, Emory, Duke, and BU are the top. And then the other ones."

Anne: "I know, and I have been wrong here in not telling you that I'm not sure what we are going to be able to afford. If you get a scholarship, great, but I don't think there is much that I can give you in terms of tuition. We can look into loans to see if we can get the rest covered, but I don't know about taking on more debt right now."

Tyler: "Don't worry. Dad is covering it, right?"

Anne: "I'm not sure. I don't know much about his finances, but he has told me that he probably can't swing the whole thing himself."

Tyler: "That's a load of BS."

Anne: "Look, your dad loves you and I really have no idea what his paycheck looks like anymore. I just know that he pays child support, so he is doing what he can. It's better for us to think about our various options here, and then you can have a separate conversation with your dad, or all three of us together."

Tyler: "So was it all a joke, trying so hard in school? I'm at a 3.8 GPA now."

Anne: "No, sweetheart, definitely not. Look, I will try to give what I can and look into loans and whatnot, but you also should investigate other schools that would cost us less, just in case. I know your school has that financial aid seminar coming up, and you can also talk to the guidance counselor. Then I'll see what I can figure out on my end."

Tyler: "Fine. But I really want those schools."

Anne: "I know, I get it. I hope it all works out, but I am hoping you understand that I am doing the best I can, and so is your dad. We are both proud of everything you've done in school and with lacrosse and we will try our best to help you, but there just isn't a lot of money right now."

Tyler: "Okay Ma."

Anne used empathy, validation, and honesty to get her point across to her son. She took responsibility for not being as forthcoming with Tyler as she should have been, and she is being open and direct right now. Far from badmouthing his dad, even when Tyler initiates this, she is overcoming her own anger and focusing on what Tyler's dad is doing right, such as paying child support. This sort of conversation doesn't ensure that Tyler gets to go to the school that he wants, but it does ensure that he knows that his mother is trying her hardest and loves him. This is even more important than going to UCLA, which Tyler will likely realize as an adult.

BE FLEXIBLE

The common theme of parenting a teenager, particularly a teenager who is dealing with a divorce, is "be flexible." If your teenager only communicates via text, learn emoticons. If your teenager doesn't talk much but likes to go shopping together, take her to the mall, at least to window shop. You don't win any points by being rigid or sticking to your guns about small things, and you have to pick your battles. However, don't err on the side of being too permissive, which will lead to resentment and stress for your child. Remember, your teenager is coping with the dissolution of the only family she has known, and this will certainly exacerbate the usual teenage drama and turmoil. Use empathy and validation to show your child that you understand her and take her seriously.

Try to focus on the fact that your teenager is only a child under your care for a few more precious years. Try to make every day (or reasonably, at least one day out of every week) one that you will remember fondly when your teenager is an adult and out of the house. Try to challenge yourself to be more tolerant and flexible than you thought you could be, but don't just abdicate the role of parent, even if your own divorce-related stressors threaten to overwhelm you. Seek counseling if you find yourself unable to be fully present for your teenager. This is a key time in child development, and no matter what is going on in your life, you need to be emotionally available for your child.

Key points from this chapter:

- Teenage years are very difficult, even without the added stressor of divorce

- Your relationship with your teenager is more important than stopping any behavior he is doing

- Acknowledge your teenager's needs and preferences, even if you don't give in to them

- It is normal for a teenager to want to spend more time with friends and significant others than with parents; don't let your teenager get out of seeing you entirely, though

- Teenagers can be dramatic and black-and-white in their thinking, and this can make them lash out viciously at one or both parents

- Try to be involved without micromanaging your child

- Owning your own mistakes and apologizing go a long way with teenagers

- Teenagers rise to the occasion: The more you respect your teen, the more mature he will act

- If you are truly scared for your teen, find her a therapist; family therapy can also help you improve your parent-child relationship

PART 3

New Challenges

Even if the early stages of the divorce are over and your children appear to be doing fine, inevitably new challenges will arise. This section covers a range of issues that may come up in the months and years after your divorce. As children grow into young adults, families will change—parents often will re-marry or find a new partner. These circumstances bring up unique challenges for divorced families as they try to cope with the emotions brought up by blending families. Additionally, we cover ways to maintain the connection that you have so carefully built with your child, at any age.

CHAPTER 12

NEW PARTNERS, NEW PROBLEMS

Approximately 60 percent of parents remarry within six years after their divorce, and the addition of a new partner or potential partner into the mix is likely to create a seismic shift in your relationship with your child. It may take a while for your child to acclimate to this new person, but there are ways to moderate the negative effects of your or your co-parent's new relationship on your child.

WHAT'S YOUR CHILD THINKING?

Your child may act very rudely to your or your co-parent's new partner, which may be entirely out of character. Your child may also detach from you, refuse to see your new partner, or regress in her behavior and become more attention-seeking. In order to understand these difficult behaviors, let's try to empathize with what your child may be thinking when she is introduced to your or your co-parent's new partner, whom we will call Jane.

"If I like Jane, I'm not being loyal to Mommy."

A child who feels this way will likely not respond much to Jane, no matter how nice and unassuming Jane is being. She may do things completely out of character, like not accept gifts or refuse to play her favorite games if Jane is involved. The child may also be outright rude to Jane, laughing at her, or telling a younger sibling not to listen to her. When acting this way, this child is often picturing Mommy at home, by herself, missing her kids, who are now here with this intruder. The child feels guilty if she likes Jane, as though doing so would directly hurt her mother. And in many cases, unfortunately, she is right.

Meanwhile, you, the person who told Jane how sweet your kids were and how well they now seem to be coping with the divorce, feel like a fool. You also feel horrible for Jane, your new girlfriend, who is trying her hardest to cater to your kids and treat them like gold, and who is being mocked and ridiculed for her efforts. You start to think of your kids as bratty, rude, and selfish.

Dad's Girlfriend Is Mean

Barbara, 46, writes: "My daughter is nine, and she comes home from her dad's house telling me that his girlfriend Mary is mean to her. This makes my blood boil. I am thinking of taking him to court and making sure that woman is nowhere near my child. What should I do?"

Dear Barbara, I can certainly see why this situation would anger you. It is very tough to think about your child being mistreated by anyone, and it adds insult to injury that it's a new woman in your co-parent's life who may be doing the mistreating. Before you do anything rash, though, I encourage you to have a heart-to-heart with your daughter about what exactly Dad's new girlfriend is doing that is so "mean." It's very common for a child, especially a girl, to ally with her mother after a divorce, and it's also common for a child to sympathize more with the parent who did not yet find a new partner. It's conceivable that your daughter thinks it will make you happy to think that Dad's new girlfriend is not that great, and saying that she is mean is also a way for your daughter to show her loyalty to you.

A good way to initiate this conversation is by saying, "I am so sorry to hear that Jane is being mean to you. That must be terrible. I know that Dad loves you a lot and that it's important to him that you're happy when you live with him. Maybe if you tell me some of the problems between you and Mary, you and I can come up with ways to make it better. I am hoping that you will be able to get along with Mary, since it would be a lot more fun with Daddy if you could have fun with Mary, too."

This introduction shows empathy and support for your child but also shows that you are in fact hoping that she gets along with Mary, and that it doesn't secretly please you to have your child hate her dad's new girlfriend. Your daughter may have only a few minor examples of Mary's "meanness," and she may be relieved that you support her having a relationship with Mary. If, of course, you do harbor resentment toward Mary and toward your daughter's father, and especially if you are secretly hoping that your daughter doesn't warm to Mary, you must do some serious introspection about the damage being caused to your daughter by her perception of these attitudes. Your daughter's life will be much easier if she can learn to get along with Mary, and even to love her, if Mary becomes a permanent part of her life. If jealousy or anger is getting in the way of you encouraging this relationship, it's a good time to seek counseling about this difficult issue.

"If Daddy gives his love to Jane, what will happen to me?"

This child sees your eyes light up when you look at Jane, and she feels ousted and, again, blindsided. For many kids, an unexpected benefit of divorce is that at least one parent tends to focus on the kids more. Often, a divorce leads to fathers spending more time as the primary caretaker, at least during their days or weekends. Now, instead of asking your son which movie he wants to see, you're asking Jane.

Your son feels marginalized and may take this out on you and Jane by acting angry or rude. This behavior also serves to get the attention back on him. This is what Dr. Fitzhugh Dodson, in his 1977 book *How to Discipline with Love (From Crib to College)*, calls "The Law of the Soggy Potato Chip." A child really wants a crisp potato chip, but if all he can get is a soggy one, he will take that over no potato chip at all. The potato chip is analogous to attention. Your child wants positive, affirming attention, but if that's not available (because it's going to Jane), he'll take your angry reprimands for his rude behavior over you entirely ignoring him.

"Daddy is going to love Jane's kids more than he loves me."

This is an obvious fear for a child of any age. Your child has recently (or not so recently) experienced a major shift in his family structure, which likely led to a great deal of insecurity, no matter how well you handled it. This insecurity about his place in the family and his relationships with each parent will now be exacerbated by the addition of other children into the mix. Watching how nicely you or your co-parent treats a new partner's children is likely to trigger a lot of jealousy in your kids, who feel like they are playing second fiddle.

"What happens if I love Jane and then she leaves, too?"

This is another obvious fear for a child of divorce. After all, if his parents' marriage ended, why would this new relationship be any different? A child with this fear may hold himself back from being too affectionate or vulnerable with Jane, so that if Jane ends up leaving his life, he does not feel too much pain.

All of these questions are very normal, and as you can see, they are easy to understand. It is likely that your child is thinking about these ideas even if he doesn't ask about them directly. We will discuss how to communicate about these questions after we look more closely at some of the common issues surrounding the introduction of a new partner into a child's life.

THE POSITIVES OF NEW PARTNERS

New partners can bring a lot of positives into your relationship with your child, and even with your co-parent. The presence of new partners for one or both co-parents can change a contentious situation into a more amicable one, because the new partner is a positive influence and gives the co-parent a new life to focus on and plan. When only one co-parent has a new partner, and the other finds someone, this can equalize the playing field and even be a source of relief for the co-parent who found a new partner first. ("Now he or she won't bother me as much, since there is something else to concentrate on.")

Young children often attach to a parent's new partner, particularly if the person is kind and patient, and does not attempt to take the other parent's place. Children thrive when their parents are calm and content, and the early stages of a new relationship are generally very happy. This honeymoon stage with a new partner may result in the parent being in the best mood the child can remember. Furthermore, with the addition of a new partner, a parent may be mobilized to do more fun activities, go on vacations, and start new rituals, like dinners together.

Children love to be in family units with lots of warm and kind people, and the new partner may have parents or children who treat your children with affection and love. The best-case scenario for your child is to be able to have one more person in her life to love and spend time with. Every new person that your child gets to know and love is another source of emotional support that can buffer your child against the stressors of the divorce. Also, every person with whom your child interacts provides another learning experience about how to relate to another personality type. These lessons will serve her well in the world later on as adults.

THE CHALLENGES OF NEW PARTNERS

At first, the introduction of a new partner often causes conflict with the other co-parent, who feels angry at the idea of a new partner being prioritized over the children, or taking up time and money that should be used for the kids. And if one co-parent has found a new love interest and the other has not, this can lead to jealousy. There is also often a suspicion that a "new" partner was actually an affair partner prior to the divorce, or this may be a known actuality. In these cases, anger and bitterness flare in the other co-parent.

Self-Compassion in Action: Dealing with a Co-Parent's New Partner

If your co-parent starts a new relationship, it is natural to feel a renewed sense of sadness. The fact that you are no longer together, and will not ever be together again, is made more salient by the appearance of this new partner on the scene. This happens irrespective of whether you know that the divorce is the right choice, and can happen in spite of conscious feelings of hatred, dislike, or indifference for your co-parent. As we discussed in Chapter 5, if you suppress your feelings of sadness, or tell yourself that you're being ridiculous, this will prevent you from processing these emotions and moving on. Additionally, your suppressed emotions may pop back up in snide comments about your co-parent's new partner, an obsession with finding out information about him or her, self-pity, and other secondary emotions, which grow out of your primary emotion of sadness.

A much healthier response would be to tell yourself, "It makes sense that I am feeling sad that my co-parent has a new partner. We spent many years together and many of them were good. I still love him on some level, I guess. It is understandable and normal that I would be feeling a sense of loss right now." Giving yourself compassionate permission to feel whatever you are feeling can be life changing. It can also be good training for being compassionate and accepting toward your children when they express emotions that are painful for you to observe, such as sadness or anger about your divorce.

While young children may attach easily to a parent's new partner, as discussed previously, older children may be curt, distant, suspicious, or even openly rude. They may have overheard their other parent's anger and suspicion about this new person, which makes them view him or her with distrust and even contempt. They may be old enough to wonder themselves about when their parent started his or her relationship with this person, and to wonder if it was while the parents were still married.

HOW TO TALK ABOUT YOUR NEW PARTNER TO YOUR CHILD

It is best to be honest with your child around the topic of your or your co-parent's new partner. Don't introduce your child to someone new until you are sure that this person will be part of your life, because it is traumatic for a child to lose a person to whom he has become close, even just for a few weeks. On the heels of the divorce, such an experience will confirm the child's greatest fear, which is that no relationship can be trusted and everyone leaves. A good time to introduce your new partner is after you have said, "I love you" and have been monogamous for at least one month. Of course, you can always wait longer, and this may be better for more sensitive or anxious children.

It would be ideal if you and your co-parent could agree on when to introduce new partners to the children. However, if your co-parent introduces a new partner to your child after only a few weeks or days of knowing the person, that is his or her choice. You can't change something once it happens, so you should try to be as positive and encouraging as possible when discussing this new person.

PROCEED WITH CAUTION

If you have found someone who interests and excites you, it is easy to think that your child will be happy for you. Unfortunately, as we've discussed, this is often not the case. Your children's reaction depends on many variables, including her relationship with you, her relationship with her co-parent, how long you've been separated or divorced, the relationship that she witnessed between you and her other parent, and the personality of your new partner, just to mention a few. If you want to increase the probability that your child will accept your new partner, you have to be sensitive about how and when you introduce him or her into your child's life.

If you have only recently separated, be cautious about introducing a new partner to your children. It's best to be single for at least a few months to keep your children from feeling confused and angry about how quickly you have moved on. Even if your marriage was dead for years and you feel like dating right away, don't be public and rub your children's noses in your new social life. Introducing a new partner before six months to a year may be difficult for many kids. Waiting until you've said "I love you" is a good marker, unless it's a whirlwind relationship where these words are uttered very early on. Some divorced parents even recommend waiting until you are engaged or planning the engagement. If a partner is not going to be around long-term, then introducing him or her to your children just increases the odds that your child will be disappointed if the relationship ends and this person disappears from your lives. This does not mean that you can't date short-term to get back into the dating scene; just date when your children are with your co-parent or a sitter.

When the time is right to introduce your new partner, have a discussion with your kids beforehand. Don't "surprise" them or have your new partner join for the initial discussion and introduction. Tell your kids that you have found someone that you love and enjoy spending time with. Describe your new partner, including his job, whether he has kids, where he lives, and what he likes to do for fun. Tell your kids that he is looking forward to meeting them, and when and where you're planning for the meeting to take place. Tell your kids that you love them and that you will still love them just as much when you are spending time with them and your partner together. Then ask if they have any questions.

Questions will differ based on the age and personality of your child, as well as how much time has passed since your divorce and your child's feelings about your co-parent. Some kids will ask if you're going to get married, or if this means you won't get back with your co-parent, or if you're going to move away. Answer all questions warmly and honestly, without going into detail that isn't age-appropriate. If your children are rude about your new partner, say, "I know you may be surprised and even angry with me for having a boyfriend, but I am not going to tolerate you being rude about John. If you ever have concerns about him or anything he does or says, you can tell me, but you can never be rude to him or about him."

Before introducing your partner to your kids, also tell your co-parent of your intentions to make this introduction, and ask for his or her input if this is at all possible given the dynamic in your relationship. It is possible that your co-parent may feel that this is too soon, in which case it would be good practice to ask when would be a better time and to try to compromise. It is possible that your co-parent's perspective is useful, and that your kids aren't ready yet. Even if you don't ask for your co-parent's input, he or she deserves to know that you'll be introducing someone new to your children. If you don't tell your co-parent, you're also setting him or her up to probe your kids with uncomfortable questions about this new person, since you're not opening the lines of communication for your co-parent to ask you any questions he or she may have.

The Introduction

When you introduce your new partner to your kids, make sure that you make it a low-key, fun interaction. Don't do it in public where your kids may feel self-conscious or awkward. Invite your new partner to your home for only a short amount of time, like for a meal and a bit of playtime or hanging out afterward. Two hours should be the maximum. If you have small kids, your partner might want to bring some special item to give them, like a little toy or a new book. For older kids, this is not necessary and can even be perceived as trying to buy their affection.

Don't engage in any physical affection with your partner in the very first meeting, and ramp this up gradually in subsequent meetings. No child is going to be comfortable seeing his parent kissing another person on the lips or cuddling with him or her on the very first meeting. After your new partner departs, talk with your kids about how it went. Say that you appreciate them meeting your new partner, and if they behaved nicely, express your appreciation for their kind behavior. Tell your children that you love them very much and that no matter who you date, they will always be your priority.

HOW TO TALK ABOUT YOUR CO-PARENT'S NEW PARTNER

This may be a touchy subject for you, but realize that if you seem uncomfortable around the idea of your co-parent's new partner, this will be obvious to your child, and will sabotage your child's ability to have a pleasant and enriching relationship with this person. The goal is to sound positive and upbeat about the addition of a new person into your child's life. Let your co-parent bring up the idea of his or her new partner with your child before you do. This way, the first impression that the child gets is from someone who is genuinely happy about this new person. It is also not your place to prepare your child to be introduced to your co-parent's new partner. Therefore, we will only discuss ways to communicate with your child after she has first met your co-parent's new partner:

- "I hear Daddy introduced you to his new girlfriend. She sounds really nice. What was your favorite thing you guys did together?" This is appropriate in a situation where your child returns from his co-parent's house in a positive or neutral mood.

- "I am happy for Mommy that she has a new person to spend time with." This is a good thing to say on your own, and also a good response if your child asks how you feel about your co-parent's new partner. Even if you don't feel that way, it would be a healthy feeling to aspire to, and sometimes saying things out loud helps you feel differently about them.

- "Kids feel a lot of things about parents' new partners, some good and some bad." As we learned in Chapter 9, this is a good communication strategy to allow your child a safe space to express ambivalent or negative emotions. This can be used if your child seems upset or openly states he is upset about the new partner. If your child genuinely seems completely enthusiastic, do not say this, as it could be perceived as trying to dampen your child's spirits or plant a seed of doubt in his mind about this new person.

- "I heard that you stayed in your room [or whatever the behavior may have been] when Dad tried to introduce you to Ann. I want to understand how you were feeling." This should be used in the context of a child having a very negative reaction to a new partner, and your co-parent, other children, or your child himself telling you about his behavior. This should be stated in a gentle and non-attacking way, with genuine curiosity about your child's experience and the desire to empathize.

HOW TO DISCUSS SEX WITH YOUR CHILD

Many children of divorce were exposed to either no open displays of physical affection between parents or, sometimes, very dysfunctional interactions, e.g., parents disappearing into the bedroom after horrible fights, or accusing one another of sexual infidelities. When a parent has a new partner, or when a parent is dating, sex may be back on the agenda. Although parents are not having sex in the child's presence, there is more open physical contact and affection. In *The Unexpected Legacy of Divorce*, the authors discuss that many children, particularly preteens and teens, are stimulated by and interested in these displays of affection and sexual energy. Preteen and teen girls in particular often engage in sexual activity at higher rates than their peers following a divorce, which may be in part due to being exposed to more passion and sexuality. Often, teens and preteens can be jealous, consciously or subconsciously, of their parent getting into a new and passionate relationship when these kids are exploring their sexuality and wish for romantic and sexual partners for themselves.

It is good practice to be sure that your sex life is not too obvious to your child. While locking a door is a signal that older children or teens may understand, it's disrespectful to your child if they overhear any sexual noises or see any caressing or fondling. You may be enamored of your new partner, and it's tempting to think that it will be healthy for your child to observe that you are really in love, as manifested by increased physical and sexual activity. Yes, sex is natural, but it is extremely difficult and confusing for your child to observe overt evidence of your newly invigorated sex life. Children can feel jealous, uncomfortable, or even competitive when viewing a parent engaging in a great deal of physical affection with a partner. The child may feel that this is not respectful to his relationship with his other parent, who may not engage in this behavior and may not even have a new partner.

It is also natural for a child, particularly an older child, to feel sexually excited by watching displays of sexual affection (even more subtle ones like open-mouthed kissing or caressing). Children, as small humans, are sexual beings—which is why they have crushes on other kids or adults, play doctor or express curiosity about other children's bodies, and touch their genitals when young or masturbate when older. It is normal and healthy for children to express curiosity and interest in sex, but being exposed to contact that is too stimulating or intense can be difficult for them. For example, when seeing a parent naked, some toddlers, preschool-age children, or school-age children will become overly focused on a parent's genitals or breasts, which is a sign that the child is old enough to be stimulated and fascinated by sex and bodies. This is why many parents, particularly opposite-sex parents, decide to stop bathing with their children when children grow out of toddlerhood.

If your child (of any age) makes comments about you touching or engaging in expressions of physical affection with a new partner, or if your child has accidentally walked in on you having sexual contact with a new partner, it's a good time to initiate a conversation about sex. You can tell your child that one way to express love is through touching, which is why you and your new partner touch each other. If your young child asks what sex is or how babies are made, you can give a straightforward response, such as:

"A man has sperm, and a woman has small eggs in her body, and when the sperm and egg meet, a baby is made. The sperm come out through the man's penis, and if the man puts his penis in the woman's vagina, the sperm can reach the eggs in her body. People only have sex when they are older and many people choose to wait until they are in love with someone. Sex is normal and healthy, but parents like to tell their own kids about sex. So, don't tell any kids at school about sex in case their parents haven't told them yet."

This is a good explanation for a school-age child. If a child asks about sex or babies before that, often you can discuss the sperm and egg without elaborating on how they meet. Note that I am not against telling even a young child about how sex occurs, but if your child repeats what you've told him at school, many parents are less liberal and may be upset if your child tells their child about sex. Therefore, I include the clause about not telling the other children, just as you would if your child learned that Santa or the tooth fairy aren't real before other children his age.

If your child expresses disgust or discomfort around the topic of sex, or when seeing physical affection between you and your new partner, use mirroring, empathy, and validation to ensure that your child feels heard and respected. Then consider whether you are being respectful of your child's boundaries. Apologize if you realize you have been excessive.

In general, only engage in forms of physical affection in front of your child that would be acceptable in public. A child does not need to hear any sounds of sex or be explicitly or implicitly told that you are going to have sex or that you have an enjoyable sex life. Often children in environments where sex is on display become promiscuous before they are ready, because their curiosity is piqued and they are fitting in with this new household norm. This can lead to a child getting into relationships that he is not emotionally ready for. Therefore, it is best to keep your expressions of physical intimacy moderate and discreet.

My Five-Year-Old Tries to Flirt with My Boyfriend

Megan, 35, writes: "I have been divorced for two years and my boyfriend moved in with me and my daughter a month ago. It sounds weird to say it, but I feel like she is trying to steal him from me. She flirts with him and asks him for kisses on the mouth, and has even slapped his butt! He is uncomfortable and always gives her a hug instead. My daughter doesn't spend much time with her dad, but she seems to want my boyfriend not as a father figure but as a boyfriend!"

Dear Megan, this situation is not that unusual. You're newly in love, and if I had to guess, your daughter may have seen you and your boyfriend engage in the behaviors that she is imitating now (butt slapping, kissing on the lips, flirting). Your daughter is obviously interested in these behaviors, and they are fascinating as well as stimulating to her. At five, she is entirely capable of having a crush, and of having romantic and sexual feelings.

Also, just because your daughter may not see her dad much, she still may want him to be her only father figure. Therefore, she is resolving any possible disloyalty in her mind by putting your boyfriend into the category of "boyfriend" and not allowing him to usurp the role of "father." Keep in mind, too, that your daughter really has no idea what's expected of her with your boyfriend. She doesn't know how little girls and their mothers' boyfriends are supposed to interact. You may think this stuff is obvious, but nothing is obvious to a child. She may think that you're modeling the appropriate way to act with "boyfriends" and she's following your lead.

I would sit down with your daughter and ask how she feels about your boyfriend. She will probably say she likes or loves him. This is when you can empathize, saying that you know he's a great guy and he loves your daughter very much, too. Then you can explain how relationships go between little girls and their mothers' boyfriends, and apologize for not having originally sat down with her and told her about these "rules."

You can tell her that while you and your boyfriend can kiss and touch because you're grownups, there are different rules for adults and kids. These rules include no kissing on the lips and no slapping butts; however, hugging and cuddling are fine. You can explain that the love you and your boyfriend share is grownup love, and the love that your boyfriend and your daughter share is family love, like the love she has with grandparents, uncles, aunts, or anyone else (you can use teachers or dance instructors or anyone else if she doesn't have much other family). Reassure her that you know your boyfriend is not her dad, and he will never replace her dad, but maybe he can be like a stepdad (but only use this term if you and your boyfriend have long-term plans to marry).

Blended Family Issues

Blended family issues can start long before a parent is remarried and/or living with a new partner's kids full-time or part-time. They start when a child is introduced to the children of a parent's new partner, which is often soon after the parent has realized that this relationship will be serious. Even the smallest and/or more easygoing child will find the interaction of her parent with a new, strange child to be initially disconcerting and threatening. Additionally, the new partner's children are feeling the same thing, and are jealous of your child laying a claim on their parent's time and affection. Both sets of children in these situations are initially wary and competitive. With careful parental mediation and awareness of the delicate nature of this situation, stepsiblings may become very close. But there also exists the possibility of continued conflict, competition, and resentment on both sides.

The best way to ameliorate blended family issues is with honesty and transparency from both parents. Parents should admit when parenting is difficult for them, and if they catch themselves favoring one child over another, they need to admit this and apologize. Parents can try to have weekly family meetings where all children's sides can be heard and validated, and to try to reach compromises that are not weighted heavily toward one child's preferences over the others'. In addition to family meetings, each parent should try to spend one-on-one time with each child and stepchild at least once a week, doing something fun. (See Chapter 14 for ideas of fun bonding activities.)

If your partner and/or your partner's children do not get along with your child, be sure that your child knows that you notice this and that the conflict does not affect your love for your child. It is very crazy-making for a child to have a parent deny and minimize obvious conflict with a stepparent (or with anyone else, for that matter). Try not to take sides in disagreements between your child and your partner, but always show your child that you love him no matter what conflicts are occurring. It's usually best for the biological parent to take the stricter role if need be. The bond between a biological parent and a child is much stronger than the new bond between a stepparent and stepchild, and can withstand a lot more conflict.

Additionally, there should be a zero-tolerance policy for sibling bullying. It may be nice to imagine that older stepkids will love to babysit younger ones, but this may not be the case. Don't put younger children into vulnerable positions where they can be teased or hurt by older ones. Take your children's complaints seriously and do not just assume that sibling or stepsibling rivalry will dissipate over time. If it doesn't, you're setting your children up for a lifetime of resentment and distance. If there continues to be conflict among your children, your partner, and/or your stepchildren, find a family counselor experienced with the unique challenges of blended families.

If you secretly are jealous of your child's involvement or potential involvement with your co-parent's new partner, take heart. Children rarely prefer a stepparent to a biological parent, as long as the biological parent has not completely rejected them. Try to view your co-parent's new partner as a new person who can love your child, like you view a teacher or camp counselor. Try to give the new partner's behavior the benefit of the doubt; if a child tells you that a stepparent or parent's new partner was mean to him, this may be because he is trying to assess what you think of the new partner yourself, or he has picked up on the fact that you dislike this new person and wants to ally with you.

Key points from this chapter:

- Your child will likely feel insecure and jealous upon meeting a parent's new partner

- There are ways to gently and considerately bring up the topic of your or your co-parent's new partner

- The way you handle initial meetings with a new partner can set the tone for his or her relationship with your kids

- Keep in mind that your children may become newly attuned to sex, and you may have to discuss this

- Blended family issues can be challenging, but never let your child doubt your love

CHAPTER 13

ONE THING AFTER ANOTHER

There are many issues aside from the introduction of a new partner that can be difficult for your child. Complex and emotional situations like custody evaluations, involvement of the police or child protective services, a child's accusations of mistreatment (by you or your co-parent), in-law stress, decisions about holidays, milestone events attended by both you and your co-parent, changes in finances, or a child engaging in risky or dangerous behavior can all throw a wrench into the precarious workings of your post-divorce family. All of these situations have the potential to create conflict between you and your co-parent, and to reopen your child's wounds from the divorce, even if he has previously appeared to have worked through most of his hurt and grief. We will go through each situation and ways to deal with your own feelings, as well as how to most effectively communicate with your child.

CUSTODY EVALUATIONS

Unfortunately, many times, co-parents cannot agree on a custody arrangement or a visitation schedule, or there are questions about parental fitness. Sometimes a custody evaluation is ordered by the court. In a custody evaluation, a mental health professional interviews your child and observes her with each parent, sometimes in the home. The professional then makes a recommendation about the custody arrangement that he or she believes would be in the best interest of the child.

A custody evaluation is a harrowing experience. The thing that is most important to you, spending time with your child, may be taken away from you. Of course, very few evaluators would recommend a child not see her parent, unless there is evidence of abuse, domestic violence, or substance abuse. But not being the primary caretaker of your child would feel like a grievous loss, and this cannot be minimized.

However, there is a more adaptive and helpful way to look at a custody evaluation. A trained professional will be giving feedback about how you and your co-parent could interact most effectively as a parenting team. This feedback is something that many parents never get. The evaluator may even recommend family or individual therapy, or parenting classes. This is a wonderful opportunity to learn exactly what type of parenting plan an expert considers best for your family. Remember, the most important thing is whether your child is happy and healthy. This is even more important than which days or times each parent sees your child.

Whether or not you agree with the evaluator's decision, it will be extremely emotionally difficult on your child if she sees you angry, scared, or desperate. Your job here is to cooperate calmly and honestly with the evaluation, but even more importantly, to show your child that there is nothing to be frightened of, and that the custody evaluation is in her best interest. Often, the evaluator recommends that a further evaluation be done later, when a child is older or circumstances change, so if you focus on working on what needs to be worked on now, you may be in a better position later to get more time with your child.

If your child will be undergoing a custody evaluation, it is important to help him understand what is happening. Younger children can be told that this nice person is going to help Mommy and Daddy with their parenting, so that they can be the best parents they can be. Older children can be told that this is a psychologist who is going to help figure out a parenting plan that Mom and Dad both agree on.

What Not to Do Before a Custody Evaluation

Overall, you should adhere to the guidelines set forth in Chapter 7, "How to Talk about Your Co-Parent." It is toxic for your child if you engage in any badmouthing of your co-parent or if you put your child in a no-win situation by instructing him to lie or to hide certain facts from the evaluator. Your child cannot be led to believe that it will be his fault in any way if the custody evaluation does not go as you hope. It's best not to express any thoughts or hopes at all about the custody evaluation, so that your child does not try to force the evaluation to go a certain way. In addition to being disingenuous, this would make your child feel horribly guilty if his "plan" was not successful.

Tell your child that the evaluator will be making whatever decision is best, and you will be happy no matter what. You can emphasize that the amount of time or which days you spend with your child is not important; what's important is that your child knows that you love him and will always enjoy any time you do get to spend together. If the child asks why the evaluation is occurring, state that someone who knows a lot about kids and parents is helping you and your co-parent figure out the best way to take care of him after the divorce.

Here are some points to keep in mind before and during a custody evaluation:

- Do *not* try to prep your child on what to say or what not to say, even if you are terrified that somehow you will be presented in a bad light.

- Do *not* tell your child that her behaviors will inform the basis of the recommendations. Instead, focus on the fact that the evaluators will be looking at a lot of information to figure out the best path for your family.

- Do *not* badmouth your co-parent to your child, or in any way make your child fear the outcome if she ends up living primarily with her other parent. Saying things like, "He barely even knows where your school is" will make your child anxious as well as defensive of the other parent. See Chapter 7, "How to Talk about Your Co-Parent."

- Do *not* make your child scared about the potential outcome of the evaluation, saying anything like, "They want to make sure you can keep living with Mommy, so make sure that you behave really well." In this example, if the evaluator decided that the child would be best off living primarily with her father, the child would likely feel extremely guilty for "messing up" and making Mommy look bad.

- Do *not* tell your child anything dramatic like "my life will end" or "I'll kill someone" if your co-parent gets custody. Don't let your child overhear you saying these sorts of things to others, either. Children are very literal, and will believe that you will die or murder someone if the custody evaluation does not go well. (If you truly feel these things, please seek counseling to help get you through this emotionally wrenching time.)

Remember, even if your custody evaluation does not have the outcome you had hoped for, please try to keep the principles in mind from the section on positive thinking in Chapter 5. Your child will learn how to think about the world from watching you adapt and cope with difficult situations. If you can make the best of disappointments, you will pass this resilience on to your child.

INVOLVEMENT OF POLICE OR CHILD PROTECTIVE SERVICES

If the police or child protective services have been called or involved with your family, it can be very difficult to remain calm when discussing this situation with your child. There was obviously some sort of domestic dispute, violence, or possible abuse that led to this involvement, and tempers and anxiety levels will be running high for both parents. It is important to explain to children why police or child protective services (CPS) came to your home, since this can be very confusing and scary for kids. For example, you can say something like, "When there is fighting or yelling between parents, the police/CPS are nice people who come to make sure that kids are okay." Apologize to your child for whatever behavior occurred that led to the police or CPS being called, such as saying, "I'm sorry that our fighting got out of hand and that someone called the police. I love you very much and I will try to make sure no fighting happens in the future."

If police or CPS have been called because of domestic violence witnessed by your child, it is essential to explain what happened so that your child can process it. Say something like, "Daddy hit Mommy and that was wrong. The police came to make sure that everything was okay." Again, as always, do not speak ill of your co-parent, even if it is your co-parent's behavior that directly led to police/CPS being called. Review Chapter 7 for more on the importance of respecting your child's relationship with your co-parent by not painting him or her as a villain, no matter what your personal feelings about your co-parent are. If your child witnessed domestic violence, it is recommended that you take her to see a child psychologist who can help your child process what was observed in an age-appropriate way.

WHEN YOUR CHILD ACCUSES YOU OR YOUR CO-PARENT OF MISTREATMENT

A nightmare for every parent is to be told by a child that his other parent perpetrated physical or sexual abuse. Abuse may have just started or it may have been going on for a while, even when your family was together, but the child may only have gotten brave enough to tell you now that you're living apart. Every accusation of this nature should be taken seriously, but you must restrain yourself from reacting instantaneously and lashing out or doing anything rash if your child levels such an accusation.

If your child tells you about any incident of abuse, it is important to remain calm but empathic. You want your child to see that you are listening. Do not interrogate your child, even if you find it almost impossible to restrain yourself. Just let your child describe what occurred. If you react with anger or disgust toward your co-parent, your child may interpret this as you being angry and disgusted with him, or he may retract his statement out of loyalty to his other parent.

As soon as you're not in your child's sight, write down the time and date and as many of your child's exact words as you can remember. This can help you if you need to press charges or get your child into treatment. Reassure your child that what happened was not his fault, and that you will ensure that he remains safe from now on.

There are some scenarios, however, that call into question the veracity of a claim of abuse. One possibility is that your child is angry at your co-parent, and his accusation is designed to hurt the other parent. Most of the time only a young child would do this, as an older child would understand how serious a topic this is and would stick to complaining about how mean and unfair his other parent is. Younger children have no idea how seriously an accusation like "Daddy hit me" will be taken, and by the time he figures this out, his shame over lying may stop him from telling the truth or even from consciously remembering that he lied. If your co-parent recently angered or disappointed your child, or started dating a new partner, it may be the case that your child is trying to retaliate in some way. It is unlikely, however, that a child would invent a scenario of sexual abuse, because it is unlikely that he would be aware of these behaviors had he not experienced them. It is more likely that an accusation of verbal or even physical abuse may be fictionalized, especially if there is a strained relationship between your child and your co-parent.

Another possibility is that your child misinterpreted something that happened and wanted you to help her figure out what really transpired. For example, if a small child walks in on her mother's new boyfriend in the bathroom, she may tell her mother that this man showed her his penis. If the father, angry about his co-parent's new relationship, allows himself to take his daughter at her word, this could cause tragic consequences for all parties involved.

Although it may be difficult, remaining calm and neutral is the only way that you can learn what really occurred. If you immediately respond with an angry or shocked expression or rage against your co-parent, or sweep up your child in a tide of comfort and sorrow, your child will immediately understand that his words were of monumental importance.

If he intentionally or unintentionally misrepresented what happened, he will feel embarrassed to go back and correct himself or say he was not telling the truth. He also may be very curious about the outcome of what he said, as it is rare for a child to elicit such a dramatic reaction from an adult. For an excellent film about a child falsely accusing a man of sexual abuse, watch *The Hunt*, a 2012 Danish film.

If, however, your child's story seems reasonable and honest, you must reach out to your attorney or mediator to discuss what your child said. It is also important to bring your child to a mental health professional who can evaluate the impact of the abuse, as well as help your child process her sadness, confusion, anger, or fear. Custody arrangements will also need to be changed. However, even (*especially*) in this horrible situation, you must remember that your child's emotional connection with the offending parent must be respected. It's much better for a child to believe that a parent was abusive because of his or her own issues and dysfunctions than it is for a child to believe abuse occurred because a parent was evil or unloving. It is not your child's fault that her parent acted hurtfully, so do not compound this hurt by bashing your co-parent, even if his or her behavior toward your child was objectively mean-spirited or harmful.

If your co-parent has in fact been abusive toward your child, turn back to Chapter 7 for a discussion about how to explain this to your child, and how to allow the relationship between your child and your co-parent to not be entirely destroyed by what has happened. Note that while this may mean discontinued contact with the abusive co-parent, a relationship may be able to be maintained in the child's own mind just by realizing that a parent loved him even though the parent acted in a very wrong and harmful way.

False Accusations of Abuse Leveled Against You

If you have found out that your child has told his other parent that you have abused him, this can be shocking and extraordinarily upsetting. But in instances of parental alienation (see Chapter 7), one parent sometimes purposely invents incidents of abuse or neglect at the hands of the other parent, and, tragically, the child begins to believe that these events took place. The child will swear up and down that a parent abused him even if prior to the other parent discussing it, he had no such memory.

A significant body of research demonstrates that children are extremely suggestible. The way that they view situations, and even the memories that they have, can be influenced by a variety of factors. The children themselves can believe wholeheartedly that situations happened, even if there is no evidence for this. The work of Elizabeth Loftus shows that false memories can be implanted in children just by having them hear an adult describe a situation that never took place. Later, the children are convinced that this event actually transpired.

There was a huge controversy in the world of psychology in the 1990s when some therapists stated that they could help clients recover repressed memories of abuse. While there is certainly evidence for repression, there is also evidence that false memories can be planted with enough suggestion, so many of these clients were being led to believe that abuse occurred when it did not. The therapists were not malicious; they genuinely felt they were helping clients realize what had happened to them. More detailed discussion of the suggestibility of children in the area of abuse can be found in *The Myth of Repressed Memory: False Memories and Allegations of Sexual Abuse* by Dr. Elizabeth Loftus and Katherine Ketcham.

If your child has accused you of abuse, you must immediately get yourself a lawyer. Many children realize later in life that a parent did not actually abuse them, but this can't happen if the relationship is entirely destroyed. For more on this topic, also read the section on parental alienation in Chapter 7.

IN-LAW ISSUES

Some lucky people remain on good terms with their co-parent's parents, but this is not the case for everyone. Sometimes your ex-in-laws can cause you more grief and stress than interacting with your co-parent does. It is normal to expect that your co-parent's relatives will be on your co-parent's side in any argument between the two of you, and some amount of coldness and rudeness may, unfortunately, be par for the course. Also, grandparents on both sides will likely "spoil" their grandchildren more during and after the divorce, which is actually very helpful for your child, as all extra love, affection, and support can act as a buffer for a child in a stressful situation. No matter how you personally feel about your ex-in-laws, it is important to try and focus on their love for your children, and to give them the benefit of the doubt if at all possible.

However, there are some situations in which it's advisable to step in and assert yourself. If your co-parent's family members are badmouthing you to your children, it is necessary to intervene. It's very stressful for your children to be placed in a situation where they are caught in the middle, wanting to defend you but not knowing how to do this without upsetting other family members they may love. Also, in extreme cases, your co-parent's relatives badmouthing you can be the first step toward parental alienation, particularly if your child has more contact with this set of relatives than he does with you. Refer to Chapter 7 for more on parental alienation.

If your co-parent's family is treating you poorly and speaking badly about you to your children, try to speak to your co-parent about it. Don't bring up old grievances and long-standing issues with these family members; stay in the present and matter-of-factly describe what has been occurring and how it makes you feel. Then ask for a concrete behavior change from your co-parent. For example, say, "Madison told me that Nana said I was 'no good.' Madison seemed upset and I was upset, too. Can you please speak to your mom about not saying that stuff about me to the kids?" If your co-parent listens, great. However, if your co-parent is unreceptive and the behavior gets worse, you may want to ask your co-parent to come to family therapy or mediation where this issue can be discussed with an objective third party.

Also, don't hesitate to stick up for yourself to your kids, without blaming or attacking. You can say, "Nana is angry that Mommy and I divorced, so she says mean things about me. It is not right for her to make you feel uncomfortable by saying that. She loves you and she is a good person, but she is saying things that are wrong. I am a good person, too, and I love you very much." You can also give your child some skills and strategies to use when she is in an uncomfortable situation, like saying, "I love you but I don't want to talk bad about Daddy," or, for a less assertive child, "Let's talk about something else, please," or even just changing the topic. Whatever you do, don't let your children hear you be bashed by other family members without standing up for yourself. Not only does this keep your kids in a tough situation, but you're missing an opportunity to show them how to stand up for themselves without sinking to an attacker's level. You are modeling confidence and assertiveness, and your child will be likelier to assert himself in the future after watching you doing so.

HOLIDAYS

Holidays can be stressful at the best of times even for happily married adults, who have to deal with competing demands from two sets of parents, financial stress around gifts, and spending extended amounts of time with difficult relatives. There is also the disconnect between your idealized expectations for the holidays and the, oftentimes, disappointing reality. For divorced parents, though, holidays can be even more stressful. There can be vicious fights over which parent (and set of grandparents) gets to spend time with the children, as well as competition over who can give the child the best gifts. The parent who is spending the holiday without the child can feel bereft, depressed, and cheated, and the parent who "gets" the child often has a hollow victory when the child misses the other parent, or when the holiday turns stressful and difficult.

Children pick up on all of these feelings in their parents, and will especially worry about the parent who will be left alone during the holiday. Holidays are times when children may mourn the loss of a non-divorced family even more, especially if they have positive memories of the family spending time together on these occasions. (Even if you did not enjoy holidays with your then-spouse, your children may have been happily unaware of your feelings.) Also, if it is their first holiday after the divorce, your kids may be extremely anxious about how it will go, which can manifest in irritability, rude behavior, and acting disengaged, in addition to more obvious expressions of worry.

It can be very tempting to make holidays into a major battle, even if they alternate. It feels like you are fighting for the right to be a parent, since holidays symbolize family and parenting to so many people. But this is a good time to use your positive thinking skills from Chapter 5. In reality, holidays are only a few days out of the year. Your child will remember your daily life with you more than who he spent which holiday with on which year. It is the small everyday interactions that comprise the bulk of parenting. Additionally, you can choose to celebrate holidays at any time you want. Christmas is often celebrated twice even in non-divorced families, so both sets of grandparents can participate. Easter egg hunts happen on many days leading up to Easter, and costume parades and trick-or-treating occur at malls and senior centers on many days aside from Halloween itself. Many adults in therapy remember vicious arguments between their parents over holidays, and always say that these were times of extreme stress and discomfort. If you have to fight with your co-parent about holidays, it means that even if you get your child for them, you may have won the battle but lost the war. Many children even end up hating holidays, both as kids and later as adults, because their parents made them occasions for guilt trips and fighting.

Holidays, like everything else, are what you make of them. In addition to focusing more on non-holiday parenting and each co-parent celebrating each holiday in his or her own way, you can also make up your own special holidays to share with your child—for example, half or even quarter birthdays, solstice days, the first day of every month, or a pet's birthday. Even better, you can research wacky or little-known holidays online and celebrate them. One list is here: *www.holidayinsights.com/moreholidays*. Preschoolers and older kids love silly holidays like Fortune Cookie Day (September 13th), National Popcorn Day (January 19th), and Teddy Bear Picnic Day (July 10th). Be creative while showing your child that life is filled with opportunities to make your own good times (see Chapter 7).

Remember, if you would like your child to continue to associate holidays with happiness and fun, it is important that you do not express your sadness, anger, or anxiety about a change in how holidays are celebrated. If your co-parent has your child for the holiday, tell your child that you have other fun plans, and actually make some other fun plans for yourself. It is not fair to you or your child for you to spend a lonely and depressing holiday by yourself, which will likely affect your mood when you next see your child. If your child knows that you are okay on your own, this allows him to enjoy his time with his co-parent and other relatives.

Additionally, if you cannot afford to buy expensive gifts for your child, just don't. It doesn't matter whether your co-parent is doing so; this is not a competition. Instead of making the holidays about how much money can be spent, take a different approach. Even young children can be taught that donating to others, such as by participating in a toy drive, is a positive way to celebrate a holiday, and you can also purchase each child a couple of small material gifts and an "experience" gift (e.g., tickets to the zoo or an ice skating rink). Teaching children to focus less on materialism is one positive benefit of having less money to spend. Parents are often very surprised by how easily children can adapt to receiving fewer or smaller-scale gifts, and how enthusiastically they learn to give to the needy, particularly if they are directly involved, e.g., by accompanying you when delivering toys to a hospital or canned goods to a food bank.

MILESTONES

It can be difficult even when happily married to negotiate both partners' viewpoints about certain major events in your child's life, which can include everything from a child's earliest birthday parties, first day of school, school plays and sporting events, to graduation, prom, and heading off to college. When parents are divorced, they may find these events to be extremely stressful, particularly if their divorce has been conflictual. Both parents have to agree on certain parameters—such as which school a child should attend or curfew at prom—and the usual negotiations become even more highly charged and contentious because of the intensity and significance of these events. This is similar to what happens during holidays, discussed in the preceding section.

Try to use your skills of empathy and validation when negotiating with your co-parent about significant events. Keep in mind that the point of these events is to make your child feel recognized and special. Any conflict between you and your co-parent will suck the joy out of these occasions for your child. Defer to your co-parent when possible on any issue about which your feelings are not very extreme. Any time that you give in, your co-parent will feel more valued and involved, and is likelier to return the kindness by giving in on issues that are more important to you. Do not aim to have equal numbers of concessions made by each party. This type of score-keeping helps nobody, least of all your child.

There is also the stressor of having to see and interact with your co-parent in a public venue during these events. It's important to keep in mind that many adult children of divorce remain extremely angry and resentful about the way their divorced parents interacted at major events. Rather than a child being able to either relax, in the case of a fun event like prom, or focus, in the case of an athletic meet or school performance, the child's attention was on his parents, and whether they would be able to get through the event without embarrassing the child. Many children also feel that their parents try to steal the spotlight and make their children's events about themselves. Some parents subconsciously may even use children's events as a stage to play out a drama with a co-parent or a venue to debut a new relationship.

Instead of making these events about you, try to work as a team with your co-parent to ensure that your child remains the focus. Try to preplan with your co-parent to limit the chances of a conflict erupting at an event. Even something as seemingly inconsequential as one co-parent not sitting next to the other at an event can be interpreted by sparring co-parents as a conscious attempt of one to humiliate the other. To avoid these sorts of dilemmas, plan ahead and try to discuss all possible expectations that each co-parent has for the other.

Here are some possible examples of questions to discuss with your co-parent about events:

- At a dance recital, if Mom is backstage, will Dad sit with Mom's parents in the audience? Is he made aware of the fact that other dads may bring flowers to their performers?

- At a graduation, will both parents go out to eat with their child after the ceremony?

- At prom, will Dad be invited to see the child off in the limo that is picking her up at Mom's house?

Lastly, remember not to bring a new partner to one of your child's events without asking your child if it is okay and without informing your co-parent ahead of time. In fact, if it is an important event, don't even ask your child; just don't take your new partner. Your child has enough to concentrate on without thinking about your new relationship.

CHANGES IN FINANCES

If you and your co-parent are struggling with the financial demands of having two households, this can change your child's lifestyle dramatically. This is difficult in and of itself, but the situation is worsened if you feel that your co-parent is purposely not contributing his or her share. Parents also often feel frustrated when a co-parent's new partner or new family "takes up" the financial resources that were previously allotted to their child.

It is reasonable for your child to feel disappointed about changes in activities, lessons, camps, or schools, and to mourn the loss of buying whatever clothes, toys, electronics, and anything else that he wanted, if this was the norm prior to the divorce. Often, in this situation, parents feel so guilty about their child's change in circumstances that they lash out and blame a child for acting "spoiled" when he complains about not having certain luxuries anymore. But this is invalidating and unfair to your child. You raised your child in whatever lifestyle he has become accustomed to, and that is not his fault. Instead of snapping at your child or complaining alongside him, tell your child that you are sorry for the change in circumstances, but it cannot be helped. Try to brainstorm ways to continue sending your child to the activities in which he is most invested. Prioritize experiences over material possessions, lessons or trips over toys or clothes. Work with your child to figure out ways to get around your financial constraints, like shopping at consignment/ thrift stores or going camping instead of another type of vacation. Positivity and resourcefulness is often remembered very fondly by kids who grew up under strained financial circumstances. This is an excellent chance to show your child how to be happy and flexible even in tough times.

Many moms also bemoan the "Disneyland Dad" phenomenon, which is the idea that dads who see their kids fewer days a week than moms do take on the "fun parent" role while the mom turns into "the enforcer." In this dynamic, moms feel that dads believe they don't have to enforce rules about homework, bedtime, healthy eating, or anything else because they see the kids so infrequently that their time together should be all positive (like how many grandparents act). Often this dynamic emerges even when dads and moms split custody down the middle, and sometimes it is gender-reversed, with a stern dad and a "lazy" mom. Here is one example of a parent struggling with this dynamic and my advice, from DivorcedMoms.com:

My Co-Parent Has No Structure for the Kids

Reader Recently Divorced writes: "I thought that being in a bad marriage with arguing, lack of connection, and no communication was going to be the worst point in my life, but it has been trumped by co-parenting. My ex and I divorced earlier this year and since then, he has done nothing but make my life a living hell. Our kids are 5 and 7 years old, and they really need a routine—sleep, healthy food, and to have a sense of structure in their lives. My ex flies by the seat of his pants, has the kids eat pizza and Chinese take-out all the time, is consistently late to drop them at school and to pick them up, and never puts them to bed on time. They are exhausted and burned out after their visits with him, and of course I have to spend at least two days just dealing with the aftermath of their visits (e.g., catching them up on homework, sleep, etc.). Nothing I say has any impact and my ex accuses me of being controlling and crazy. Help!"

Dear Recently Divorced, I'm sorry you're going through this difficult time, and I empathize with you. Many parents, especially mothers, worry about the effects of lack of structure on their children, and prioritize sleep, nutrition, and stable routines above all else. (It is rare in my personal or professional experience to see a dad who is as obsessed as a mom with kids' mealtime and bedtime schedules.) Further, your divorce is recent, so the stress may feel overwhelming. And you're still acclimating to not having your kids with you all the time. To think of your kids as unsafe or neglected in any way will obviously exacerbate your sadness and anxiety about not being with them.

However, it does not seem like your co-parent is necessarily doing anything neglectful or dangerous, although he may fit the common "Disneyland Dad" stereotype. There is far more data on the negative effects on children of high conflict between divorced parents than on the effects of eating pizza three times a week, or not doing second grade homework. Being exposed to conflict in any form is toxic to kids, and it's unlikely you're able to completely shield your children from what you think about their dad's parenting style. This is going to make your kids feel terrible; they don't know who to side with and they feel caught in the middle.

Kids who see their parents arguing, or who sense tension between their parents, are caught in a very bad position. They often feel that they must ally with one parent or the other, and feel guilty about spending time with one parent and leaving the other. They take on responsibility for the conflict and often assume it centers on them and their bad behavior. This guilt can manifest in bad behavior and emotional problems.

You owe it to your kids to try to accept that your ex's way of parenting is just that, his way, and although you don't personally agree with it, it seems unlikely that arguing with him is going to change much. So you have two choices:

1. Your ex keeps doing what he's doing and your kids are also exposed to conflict about it.

2. Your ex keeps doing what he's doing and your kids are exposed to no conflict about it.

Number two seems like the clear winner, although it is no easy task and will certainly take self-awareness and restraint. I have many clients whose parents divorced, and none of them ever have complained about being fed Chinese take-out or going to bed late. They do, however, have long-lasting feelings of sadness, anger, and bitterness if they felt they were caught in a no-win situation, had to choose sides, or ended up having no relationship with one parent at the behest of the other.

I know this isn't happening now, but your kids are still young. They may soon realize how upset you are at the arrangement and start protesting going to Dad's house in order to keep you happy. This would be winning the regular-sleep-routine-and-food battle, but losing the kids-having-two-healthy-parental-relationships war.

I encourage you to keep doing what you're doing in terms of stability, routine, healthy meals, regular bedtimes, and so forth but to just completely ignore what your co-parent does with the kids, unless it is either abusive or truly dangerous. When you see their father during drop-offs, see if you can try hard to visualize him as the fun guy that your kids love, and who is probably trying to be a good dad in his own way.

He's probably also reeling from the divorce just as you are, even if it doesn't seem like it. Focusing on his positives as a dad can help you put a smile on your face and say, "Have a great weekend." When he realizes you're no longer going to criticize him, your kids' dad may even start respecting your perspective more on parenting decisions.

Also, there is a possibility that he will agree to see a counselor that specializes in co-parenting after divorce, even if only to get someone else to agree with him that you're "crazy and controlling" (this is highly unlikely; the counselor would instead try to help you communicate better and find compromises). Whether or not he consents to trying this, you yourself would likely benefit from seeing a therapist to explore and process the anger and grief over your divorce and subsequent parenting and co-parenting challenges.

WORST NIGHTMARE: RISKY BEHAVIORS

Some preteens and many more teenagers start to explore dangerous behaviors, such as drinking, smoking, drug use, and sexual activity. These behaviors are every parent's worst nightmare, particularly divorced parents who already feel guilty about potentially harming their children. It does no good to overreact, cry, yell, or punish your child if you discover evidence of these activities, and just because your child is experimenting with dangerous behaviors does not necessarily mean that something is "wrong" with your child.

Sometimes these behaviors are coping strategies for dealing with feelings of low self-worth, depression, and anxiety. Other times, children are just exploring what they may see certain peers doing. And sometimes, a child is engaging in these behaviors because she is left alone more than she is used to, which is often unavoidable as finances change post-divorce and require many people to increase their work hours. Children in this position may feel that nobody cares about them enough to supervise them, so either purposely or by default, they will begin to hang out more with peers who engage in more risky behaviors. Your course of action should be based upon the reason that you feel that your child is acting out, and you can't assess the reasons without talking honestly and openly to your child.

Before confronting your child about her risky behaviors, try, if at all possible, to have a discussion with your co-parent. You would certainly want your co-parent to inform you and ask for your input in a situation where your child was engaging in dangerous activities without your knowledge. Give your co-parent the same respect, whether or not you feel you will agree with his or her perspective. Ask for your co-parent's opinion, using the curiosity that we learned in Chapter 5. Respond to your co-parent's feelings and reactions, which may include anger, sadness, or minimization (e.g., saying, "I used to drink in high school, what's the big deal?") with empathy or at least neutrality. Do not blame your co-parent's parenting style for the behaviors that your child is currently exhibiting. This will anger your co-parent, and instead of working together as a team on this issue, you'll end up attacking one another.

Both you and your co-parent should have a meeting with your child to discuss the concerning behavior. If you and your co-parent get along, you can have this meeting together, which is preferable since this shows your child that both parents are on the same page and seriously concerned. If you don't get along well enough for this, have individual meetings. When you sit down to talk to your child, do not allow your panic to push you to berate, ground, or threaten your child. Look at your child's behavior as a call for help and attention. Use it as an opportunity to show that you can in fact be trusted not to fly off the handle, even in challenging situations. You want your child to be able to come to you with any problems, and if you act shocked, enraged, personally hurt, or any other extreme emotion, your child will just think that you are so fragile or volatile that you have to be handled cautiously, rather than used as a support.

Therefore, use the communication skills you learned in Chapter 6 to start a calm discussion about whatever you have discovered, using curiosity and empathy. Ask your child how he is feeling and why he thinks he is doing these activities. Be ready for your child to minimize them, saying, "Everyone was drinking at the party, not just me." Don't attack your child or try to "prove" he is wrong, e.g., "I know for a fact that your sister didn't drink!" Instead, continue to express warm concern for your child. Ask about the extent of your child's engagement in these behaviors, and be sure to tell your child that his honesty will not be punished. If your child confides anything in you, empathize and validate his experience and feelings. Remember that you are trying to understand your child, not act self-righteous or holier-than-thou. Therefore, if you engaged in risky behaviors at a similar age, your child may find it useful to hear (even in a limited way) about your experiences; this makes you seem on the same team, rather than you looking down on your child for disappointing you.

Then, it's your turn to express your thoughts about your child's behaviors. You can express worry, but if you act dramatic and catastrophize, like saying that your child won't get into college if he smokes marijuana a few times, you are limiting your credibility and your child will no longer listen to your input. Try to speak in a calm, reasoned, loving way about your concerns. For example, you could say, "I found marijuana in your room and it concerns me. I know you are doing well in school, but it's illegal to smoke pot and you could get in trouble. I'm also worried that you drive while you're smoking. I love you and I'm worried about you."

Whether or not your child agrees to stop the concerning behavior, you should still have a plan in place for what you and your co-parent will do if the behavior doesn't stop. You can tell this to your child, but not in a punitive way. For example, you can say, "Dad and I would like your word that if you smoke pot, you will not drive or get into the car with anyone who has been smoking. If we find out that you've done this, we will consider taking away your driving privileges, because you wouldn't be safe on the road. In that case, we also think you would need to start seeing a counselor to talk about how you're coping."

If you have noticed that your child is depressed, anxious, irritable, or angry, he may be turning to risky behaviors as a form of self-medication; such behaviors release dopamine in the brain and make people feel temporarily better. Also, adolescents are very susceptible to peer pressure and he may have an increased insecurity about fitting in as a result of the divorce. Try, if at all possible, to spend more time with your child, or to get your child involved in other activities that could exert a positive influence (e.g., sports, martial arts, art classes). Also, after discussion with your co-parent, try to find a counselor for your child that she trusts. This should probably not be the school counselor, because your child may not feel comfortable confiding in someone who "may tell the teachers" or who other students observe that she is going to see. Try to find a psychologist who works with adolescents, and who is able to connect with your child in initial sessions. Additionally, if your interactions with your child continue to escalate over risky behavior, family therapy can be wonderful for helping you and your child learn to communicate better.

CHAPTER 14

KEEP ON KEEPIN' ON

After incorporating the techniques you learned in this book for connecting with your child, you will likely feel much more positive about your parenting and your relationship with your child. You will feel more confident in your ability to help your child weather the emotional ups and downs of your divorce. Yet, no matter how well you understand your child, no matter how well you communicate, and no matter how many opportunities for bonding you create, things will change over time. Different issues crop up over weeks, months, and years, including moves, new jobs, new relationships/families, illness, job loss, death in the family, and so on. It's important to have a routine in place for keeping the lines of communication open with your child, even as life throws obstacles in your way.

MAKING YOURSELF AVAILABLE

It's important to keep checking in to see how your child is doing emotionally, even months or years after the divorce. This is important in non-divorced families as well. By advising you to check in and see how your child is feeling, I don't mean to say that you should hover over your child and anxiously inquire about his psychological health. As we've discussed, many children do best when they can choose when to approach you with questions or topics of conversation. Your job is to make yourself available, physically and emotionally.

One good way to make yourself available is to set up both daily and weekly times for spending individual time with each of your children. If you have two very small kids, you can set one up with TV or some sort of game while the other sits with you. It is important that you don't always treat siblings as a unit, no matter how overwhelmed you feel, but have individual time with each child. Most children with siblings greatly value individual time, since it's hard to come by, and they can relax and not have to compete for parental attention.

You'll have two types of daily time together: check-ins and special time.

Check-ins

Check-ins are for preschoolers and older kids. Toddlers don't really understand check-ins, and thrive more on special time, which we discuss in the next section. For check-ins, you should try to take at least 10 minutes to be fully attentive to and engaged with your child when you first see him after school. Even though this can be a hectic time, especially if you're coming home from work and have to race to make dinner, do homework with your child, and catch up on everything else you have to do, it is worth it in the long run to show your child that he is your number-one priority. Tell your child that this is time for you and him to talk, and start out by asking something like, "So, how was your day?" Children love to know what's coming, and they will come to rely on this little ritual, knowing that this is their time to connect with you if they have something to discuss. Calling this a check-in, or any other name you come up with, can help make this into a focal point of your daily routine.

In a best-case scenario, your check-in with each child should be in a calm place and away from the demands of other children, so you can make eye contact with your child, put away your phone, and sit close. But make do with the time you have. Some parents use ten minutes during bedtime to talk to their kids and some use dinnertime. You can even use your drive home to talk with your child, if that's all that you have. Preteens or teens may be able to talk most freely on the phone, if you call from work when they are already home from school. In the case of a very busy teen and a working parent, you can do this via text some days. Be creative. The more you're committed to having a daily check-in, the more your child will see how important he is to you.

Furthermore, if a child knows that you are available for talking, and that he will have your complete attention, he will approach you when he wants to talk about issues that upset or confuse him. But if a child feels that you're always busy, or half-paying attention, he will turn away from you emotionally to avoid getting rejected. Many children of divorce feel abandoned by parents who emotionally withdraw from them due to their increased stress levels and preoccupation with financial, logistical, and other issues. This is common, but it doesn't have to happen to you and your child. Even a few minutes of one-on-one time with each of your kids each day will make a tremendous difference in their relationships with you and their self-esteem.

Special Time

In addition to your daily check-ins, it is ideal to also set aside 10 minutes a night for "Special Time with Mommy/Daddy," which older kids or teens can just refer to as "hanging out." This can also be an hour per child per week, and you can do it in one full hour on the weekend if your nights and mornings are too crunched. Nothing fancy needs to happen during these times together, but they need to occur regularly so that your child knows that you and she will have time to just hang out and have fun. This is particularly important after a divorce, when the general atmosphere is often very tense. Incorporating special time into your daily or weekly routine can often help improve children's behavior, since many times when kids act out, they are hoping to get their parents' attention. If they are confident that they will get regular amounts of attention on a predictable schedule, they often feel calmer.

Here are some ideas for special time with young children:

- Walk around the block
- Go to the playground
- Rock collecting in the backyard or park
- Shell collecting on the beach
- Library time
- Frozen yogurt or ice cream shop
- Lunch at a restaurant or a picnic
- Helping you garden
- Helping you cook
- Playing with Play-Doh
- Coloring
- Playing dolls
- Solving puzzles
- Pretend play
- Listening to music and dancing
- Making a collage
- Making cards for family members' birthdays or for holidays
- Playing guessing games, like "Guess the animal I'm thinking of" or "I Spy"
- Taking a train or a bus, just for fun
- Feeding ducks, pigeons, or squirrels

For older children, preteens, or teenagers, activities can include:

- Going to a movie
- Manicure/hair salon
- Going to a sporting event
- Miniature golf
- Bowling
- Going to the mall
- Drawing together
- Beading
- Helping your child organize or add to any collections
- Building things out of LEGOs, popsicle sticks, etc.
- Cooking together
- Biking
- Visiting a museum
- Going to the zoo or aquarium
- Playing ball
- Painting pottery
- Crafting
- Running or walking together
- Going to the gym together
- Lunch or dinner
- Concerts
- Watching movies and TV
- Playing video games together
- Reading and discussing books together

The point of these activities is to be an oasis of fun and connection for you and your child even during difficult times. Don't become fixated on the educational value of the activities; they are just for enjoyment and bonding. As Forehand and Long suggest in *Parenting the Strong-Willed Child: The Clinically Proven Five-Week Program for Parents of Two-to Six-Year-Olds*, refrain from teaching, asking questions, or in any way detracting from the enjoyment of this special activity by trying to imbue it with secondary value as a teachable moment. For example, if you're playing with your three-year-old, don't ask, "What noise does the cow make?" as you play with farm toys. Instead, just say, "Mooo!" when you pick up the cow, or just smile and laugh. And with a teen, don't say, "I guess John didn't think about what would happen if he drove drunk" after you watch a movie. Just talk to your teen the same way you would talk about the movie to a friend.

This doesn't mean that you shouldn't use shows or books as jumping-off points for interesting conversations. For example, characters on the show *Degrassi* struggle with many middle-school and teenage issues, and these can be excellent ways to start discussing sensitive topics with your kids, if you're careful not to try to push your agenda during these talks. Children are very sensitive to feeling manipulated, and if you use books and TV as a way to bring the conversation around to things that you disapprove of, you're going to stop any feelings of warmth and closeness in their tracks.

Also, don't force conversations during these activities. Some kids express love and closeness verbally, and some kids just like to be engaged in an activity together. Don't assume that if you like to process your feelings verbally, your child is the same way. Open enjoyment of your child and spending time with him is the best way to inoculate him against many of the stressful feelings associated with the divorce.

SHOWING YOUR LOVE

It is important to take little bits of time to show your child that you think about her even when you're very busy. During a divorce and as a single parent, you likely don't have a lot of time or energy, but just taking a few minutes out of the day to make a small, loving gesture to your child can go a long way in making her feel loved and valued. This also increases the likelihood that your child will trust you and come to you when she is feeling down and sad.

Quick Ways to Show Small Kids That You Love Them

Here are some easy and quick ideas for ways to show toddlers through elementary-school-age children that you love them.

1. **Surprise notes:** For toddlers or preschoolers, you can just draw a cute little picture. A big hit is drawing yourself and your child together. Place notes anywhere—under his breakfast plate, in his coat pocket, in his car seat, on his pillow, on top of his toothbrush, folded inside his cereal bowl, or inside his lunch box.

2. **Pipe cleaner people:** Even the most artistically challenged person can twist a pipe cleaner into something that looks like a person, or an animal, a flower, or a heart. If not, you can at least make a bracelet! This is another little item that can remind a child that you love her during her day.

3. **Stickers:** Put a sticker of your child's favorite character on his shirt, and say that whenever he sees it during the day, he can remember that you love him. Stickers are cheap, so buy them in bulk.

4. **"Tattoo":** With a nontoxic marker, you can draw your child a special little picture, or just "I love you" on the inside of her arm. Tell her that this is a special tattoo that shows everyone how much you love her, or for a shyer child, draw a little picture or secret symbol. Tell her that this is a secret tattoo that only you two know about, and that it means you love her. You can also have your child draw a matching tattoo on your arm.

5. **Voicemail:** You can record a voicemail in your own voicemail box of you talking to your child and saying you love him. Then you can give your phone to your child, telling him he has a message. Kids get a kick out of this and want to listen to it over and over. Another option is to record a video of you at work or at home talking to your child, and show it to him later that day.

6. **Kiss box:** This is an empty box that your child can decorate. You can put a kiss "into" it when you leave for work or to go out. Tell your child that if she misses you, she can open the box and take out a kiss. There is a great picture book, *The Kiss Box* by Bonnie Verburg, that you can read with your child if the kiss box idea is a hit.

7. **Special code:** You make up a special code with your child that means "I love you." Try a secret wave or your fingers touching. Your child will enjoy thinking up her own special code, and whenever one of you does the signal, the other should respond. Different parents and sibling pairs can all make up their own special codes.

8. **Special book:** Designate one of your child's favorite short picture books as your special book. Before bed, no matter if you read other books or not (of course, the more reading, the better!), always read your special book, too.

9. **Special spy names:** You can make up secret spy names with your child, like Red Turtle or Dancing Flamingo. The sillier the better. Only you two know the secret names, so your child will feel special. If your child likes this idea, read the book *006 and a Half: A Daisy Book* by Kes Gray.

10. **Special language:** Make up your own words for hello, goodbye, and I love you. They can be in a real language or one that you and your child invent.

11. **Special song:** Make up a little song for your child based on a melody you love, that is only for you and her. For example: "You are my Clara, my only Clara, you make me happy when skies are

gray, you'll never know dear, how much Mommy loves you, please don't take my Clara Bear away."

12. **Journal:** Let your child pick out a special notebook at the drug store. Every day, write down what he says his favorite thing was that he did that day. Your child will be able to read this over later in life and will cherish it, and best of all, it literally only takes a minute or less each day. If you get into the routine of doing this at the same time every day, like dinner time, it will be easy to remember.

Special Things Shouldn't Hurt the Other Parent

Some children, particularly those who are sensitive, may get upset at their other parent's house if you have packed them a surprise note or special item in their suitcase or bag. Try to keep these special things for only your house, during your child's time with you. It is important to respect your co-parent's time with your child, and not to do anything that may, even unintentionally, make your child miss you even more and become upset during his time with their other parent.

Of course, there are some children who would enjoy having a special reminder of each parent when with the other. The easiest way to figure this out is to run this idea by your co-parent, and if he or she is on board, to ask your child whether he would like both you and your co-parent to give him something special to keep with him when he is at his other house. As usual, the rule is to respect your child's individual preferences whenever possible, and show him that both you and your co-parent respect each other and your child's love for both of you.

Make sure to examine your motivations closely when engaging in a special activity with your child. If you mention that your co-parent doesn't do these sorts of activities, or in some way use the special activity to compete with your co-parent, this can be very difficult on your child. Similarly, don't only engage in these activities as a substitute for spending enough everyday regular time with your child or to show off to your co-parent. The point of showing your child you love her is just that—to show that you love her, not to show what a good parent you are to outside observers or your child's other parent.

Quick Ways to Show Preteens and Teens That You Love Them

Preteens and teenagers can be difficult and distant. Still, with most kids you'll see glimpses of the loving kids they still are in their hearts. It can also be hard to spend time with kids of this age, between their busy schedules, the time they spend with your co-parent, and your own obligations. Still, the more you try to connect, the more you'll see your kids thrive and flourish. Here are some small things to do to show a middle-school- or high-school-age child that you love her. All of them take only a few minutes but demonstrate that you're thinking about your child and that she is important to you:

1. **Write a note:** Write your child a funny note with a funny drawing. Your child may call you corny or cheesy but may secretly like it. Some kids will start writing notes back, and this can be a way to communicate with a child who doesn't talk much.

2. **Musical influence:** Let your child pick out the music you listen to in the car, without criticizing it. Try to be open-minded, and if you end up liking it, thank your child for introducing it to you. You could also share some music you used to like when you were your child's age, and ask her thoughts.

3. **Baby picture:** Put a picture of your child as a baby in his room on his pillow, with a note about how cute it is. Say, "You might be big, but you're still my baby!"

4. **Send an article:** Email your child a funny article with the note: "Thought you'd laugh at this!" For a more serious child or older teenager, you could also send something relevant from the news and ask her opinion.

5. **Texting:** Text message your child that you miss and love her, not just the usual text asking where she is. Text anything that might start a conversation but that is light-hearted. Be creative and don't be afraid to be silly. Some ideas are: send a picture

of your lunch and ask if it looks good, send a picture of your office and ask if you should paint it red or blue, send a picture of your car and ask if it's the coolest car in the parking lot.

6. **Movie night:** Plan a movie night with popcorn and hot chocolate, just you and your child. Pick a movie you both like, but if that's impossible, defer to your child. Put down your phone and really watch.

7. **Ask for advice:** Ask your child's advice or input on something that might make her feel important, like which outfit you should wear to work, or what spices to use in a new dish, or what sort of features you should look for in your next car. Tailor your question to what you know your child is good at or wants to be good at.

8. **Overheard compliment:** Let your child overhear you telling someone else what a great person he is. This often means a lot more to a child than a compliment you state directly, since the child assumes it's more genuine.

9. **Take one for the team:** Let your child win at something. If he is great at video games, and you're not, play with him anyway. Make a big deal out of how bad you are, to make him laugh and feel good.

10. **Small gifts:** Getting your child a new pair of socks, a smoothie, a hair band, a pair of cheap sunglasses, or anything else that will make her smile is an easy way to show you're thinking about her when you're out shopping for any other reason.

Love Languages

One interesting way to figure out which of these will resonate most with your child is to read *The Five Love Languages of Children by Gary Chapman and Ross Campbell* and *The Five Love Languages of Teenagers: The Secret to Loving Teens Effectively* by Gary Chapman. Overall, the idea is that there are five languages of love—Quality Time, Gifts, Acts of Service, Physical Touch, and Words of Affirmation—and everyone responds to some of these more than others. So, if your child really appreciates physical touch, you know you need to hug him to show your love. But if your child loves little gifts, quality time, or words of affirmation, then use some of the previously listed ideas.

Taking a quiz about love languages with or for your child is another way to fully empathize with his experience. The way that you value others showing you their love may not be what your child considers meaningful. For example, if you value quality time but your child values words of affirmation, you may continue to push for time together every weekend, which interferes with activities that your child enjoys, like sports or hanging out with friends. This may lead to conflict, especially as a child ages. If you are aware that your child's love language is words of affirmation, then you might stop pushing for displays of physical affection, and instead might have more frequent phone conversations where you tell your child how proud you are of him and how much you love him.

PREPARE FOR CHALLENGES

If you've read this book, your goals are likely to communicate in a healthy way with your child, to protect your child from as many negative effects of divorce as you can, and to be a present and loving parent. These are wonderful and admirable aspirations, and it would be great if your behavior reflected them every single day. However, this is very unlikely to happen. There are many ups and downs, challenges, and stressors that can erode your confidence as a parent if you're not prepared for them.

Many people think that the best way to reach your goals is to be unfailingly optimistic and positive. Instead, research by psychologist Gabriele Oettingen shows that a better predictor of success at sticking to a goal is being a realistic optimist—balancing your self-confidence with the knowledge that it will be difficult to stick to your goals over time, and that you'll face struggles along the way. Other research indicates that it's easier to stick to concrete, discrete, and specific goals than intangible, general, and vague ones. And don't forget to come up with a plan for what happens when you don't meet your goals one day. Creating a realistic "plan B" for when you're feeling overwhelmed is another excellent way to increase your likelihood of parenting well during the tough time of your divorce.

During times of major stress, and even times of minor stress (which feel major at the time!), your parenting and your relationship with your child may revert to patterns that you don't like, such as not spending enough time with your child, minimizing your child's feelings, talking badly about or openly arguing with your co-parent, not setting aside time for self-care, or confiding too openly in your child. All of these tendencies can be combated most effectively just by planning for them.

Let's take an example of a newly separated mother of a four-year-old girl who has just read this book. Her co-parent was unfaithful and she expects an acrimonious divorce. Rather than thinking, "No matter what, I'll communicate better with my daughter and we'll be closer than ever after the divorce," it would be more adaptive for her to think, "I'll have ups and downs throughout this divorce process, and I can picture being very emotional and stressed at times. Still, I can commit to spending fifteen minutes a day, five days a week, talking to my daughter one-on-one and using my mirroring, empathy, and validation skills. Additionally, if I realize that I'm being invalidating or that I'm burdening her with my stress, I will commit to saying I'm sorry. I'll then resume counseling with the therapist I used to see, and I'll ask my mother for more support with child care." In this second scenario, she is being a realistic optimist, setting measurable, actionable goals, using self-compassion, and coming up with a safety net in case she finds herself struggling. This will allow her to be the best mother she can be, no matter how difficult and stressful her life may become in the near future.

Key points from this chapter:

- Check-ins and daily special time with your children can make them feel loved and cherished even when you're busy and stressed

- Have fun with your child; not everything is a teachable moment

- There are many small ways to show your love to your child

- Be a realistic optimist about your ability to parent well through your divorce

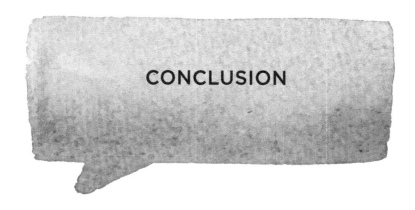

CONCLUSION

Divorce is a heartbreaking experience for all involved, but that doesn't mean that your children are doomed to sadness and misery for years to come. Your ability to communicate openly, lovingly, and honestly with your children can buffer them against a lot of the pain surrounding the divorce. The most painful memories of adult children of divorce include having their feelings ignored, having to act as an adult instead of a child, and feeling the need to choose between parents. If you respect your child's childhood and your co-parent's role as a co-parent, you will be far ahead of the game.

Although your child may be very difficult to deal with during and after the divorce, keep in mind that he is struggling mightily with grief, anger, sadness, resentment, fear, confusion, and any other emotion you can imagine. Children are distressed by divorce in most if not all cases, but they are resilient and can adapt and flourish in the changed circumstances, especially if you are a source of comfort, unconditional love, and understanding.

The most important skills to use to communicate with your child are empathy and validation. Practice these skills with your child and with others in your daily life. Every time that you validate your child instead of dismissing or denying her feelings is another feather in your cap as a parent. You are teaching your child to accept and value her own emotions, and helping her process them and move on. Emotional awareness and acceptance underlie psychological and emotional well being, and they are taught primarily at home.

Of course, no parent is perfect, and at times, you will struggle with being patient, empathic, and validating. You may sometimes still speak of your co-parent with anger and frustration within your child's earshot. Your anger, sadness, and anxiety will likely color your daily parenting, no matter how strenuously you try to separate your divorce stress from your time with your kids. When you find yourself struggling in these ways, please re-read this book, or at least the chapters on emotions and self-compassion, and try again to take a deep breath and re-connect with your child in a positive way. If you have one bad day, it does not mean that you've scarred or traumatized your child. What makes you a good parent is the ability to accept that you are only human, recoup, and try again to be the parent that you know your child needs and deserves.

Ensuring that your children know that you love them, that the divorce has nothing to do with them, and, most importantly, that you will always be there for them, willing and ready to listen to their thoughts and feelings, is a wonderful gift to give to your child. In fact, some parents find that their divorce allowed them to really focus for the first time on the specifics of their communication style and their parenting. Knowing that your child truly needs you can be a motivator for parents to try their hardest to be emotionally open, receptive, and non-judgmental—skills that they previously may not have had. If this is the case, then the divorce is a blessing in disguise.

If you try your hardest to communicate and connect with your children, even when they are frustrating and challenging, they will remember and value your efforts. The communication skills you have learned in this book will pave the way for you to help your child cope and even thrive post-divorce. While divorce is the end of one family, it can also be seen as the beginning of two new ones, each headed by one co-parent, both with the goal of keeping their children healthy, safe, and happy. Start these new families off on the right foot, with empathy, validation, open communication, and, of course, lots of love.

INDEX

ABOUT THE AUTHOR

Dr. Samantha Rodman is a clinical psychologist in private practice in Maryland, where she lives with her husband and three children. She founded DrPsychMom.com, which includes articles about psychology, parenting, and relationships. Dr. Rodman has written for the *New York Times*, the *Washington Post*, the *Huffington Post*, Babble, Psych Central, and others. She invites you to connect with her on Facebook, Twitter @DrPsychMom, and on DrPsychMom.com.